RHYMES AND RHYTHM

A poem-based course for
English pronunciation

Michael Vaughan-Rees

First published 1994

Published by MACMILLAN PUBLISHERS LTD

ISBN 0-333-59265-4

Produced by AMR for Macmillan Publishers Ltd

Illustrations by Bill Piggins

Printed in Hong Kong

A catalogue record for this book is available from The British Library.

Acknowledgements

An earlier version of Rhymes and Rhythm appeared in 1991 as a special issue of Speak Out!, the newsletter/journal of the IATEFL Pronunciation Special Interest Group. It would not have been possible without the following people and organisations, whom I would now like to thank:

- The main committee of IATEFL (The International Association of Teachers of English as a Foreign Language), in particular the then Chair, Alan Maley; for help and encouragement.

- The British Council, for buying a large number of copies for distribution around the world.

- Eurocentres, my employers, and in particular John Andrews, Principal of Eurocentre Lee Green; for providing facilities, especially for recording the original tape.

- The many people who provided help and advice, especially those who allowed their own work to be used: in particular, Ian Dunlop, Martin Glynn, Brita Haycraft, Alan Maley and David Orme.

- My Lee Green colleagues who supplied the original voices: Ian Anderson, John Andrews, Jo Van Waskowski and Mary Williams. Mick Dunn, technician extraordinaire, who made the original recording.

The author and publisher also wish to thank the following who have kindly given permission for the use of copyright material:

Alan Maley for 'My father's job's more important than yours' (page 100), 'Light and shadows' (page 101) and 'Mornings' (page 117).

Punch Library at The Express newspaper for 'Noise' by Jessie Pope (page 116).

Harper/Collins Publishers for 'Windy nights' by Rodney Bennett from The Play Way of Speech Training (page 118).

Pitman Publishing for 'Rush hour' by Maisie Cobby from Songs and Marching Tunes (page 118) and 'Look out' by Paul Edmonds from We Play and Grow (page 118).

Ian Dunlop for 'Our big steeple clock' (page 118) and 'Three seasons' (page 119).

David Orme for 'Slinky Hank the railway rat' (page 120), 'How they brought the pizzas from Brent to Penge' (page 123) and 'A car called Heapsville' (page 125).

Oxford University press for 'Victoria' by Eleanor Farjeon from A Puffin Quartet of Poems (page 121).

Peters, Fraser and Dunlop for 'The catch' by Kit Wright from Hot Dog and other poems (page 127) and 'Sky in the Pie' by Roger McGough (page 135).

Stephen Hirtenstein for 'Run, then. Run!' (page 127).

Random House UK Ltd for 'Tarantella' by Hilaire Belloc from Complete Verse (page 128).

Martin Glynn for 'Descriptive word rhythm' (page 136).

Every effort has been made to trace all the copyright holders but if any have been inadvertently overlooked, the publishers will be pleased to make the necessary arrangement at the first opportunity.

Contents

General introduction

This book uses a variety of different types of poem to make it easier for the learner of English to understand spoken English and also to be understood better by native speakers of English. The poems range from very traditional forms, the **limerick** for example, to contemporary forms such as the **rap**. But whatever the type of poem, they have something in common: they all **rhyme**, and they all have a regular **metre** (that is to say, a regular **beat** or **rhythm**).

This means two things: firstly, they are easy to repeat and remember; secondly, they can follow the natural rhythm of spoken English. This second point is very important, since English – unlike many languages – depends on a fairly regular beat going from stressed syllable to stressed syllable. You have to make sure to stress the correct syllables, since mistakes of stress are the main reason why a person may be difficult to understand.

The main beats in the poems in this book always correspond to stressed syllables. This means that if you keep to the beat, then you automatically stress the correct syllables. Take the beginning of two of the poems, each with the same ONE two three, ONE two three beat:

---

1 **Nor**man's from **Not**tingham, **Mar**tin's from **Mo**ttingham,
   Charley's from **Ches**ter and **Les**ley's from **Lee**;
   Joyce is from **Jar**row and **Hen**ry's from **Har**row,
   Laura's from **Leic**ester and **Dave's** from Dun**dee**.

2 **Ti**na's a **tea**cher, Pris**cil**la's a **prea**cher,
   Donald's a **doc**tor and **Ted** drives a **truck**.
   Fred's a photographer, **Joe's** a ge**og**rapher;
   Barry's a **bar**rister **down** on his **luck**.

The main beat (the ONE of the ONE two three) is marked in **bold**. Keep to that beat and you soon become aware that the majority of 2-syllable nouns are stressed on the first syllable. Not only that: you are forced, for example, to realise that *Leicester* has only two syllables (like *Laura*, *Charley*, *teacher*, *doctor*), that *Dundee* (unusually) has the stress on the second syllable, and that *photographer* and *geographer* have the main stress on the second syllable. And the regular rhyme scheme tells you, for example, that *Leicester* rhymes with *Chester*.

Now look at another extract:

---

3 **Per**cy per**sua**ded the **troops** to sur**ren**der
   Betty be**came** a quite **fa**mous ce**leb**rity
   Colin col**lec**ted some **mar**vellous **fur**niture
   Avril a**ver**ted a **ma**jor ca**tas**trophe

This time the beat forces you to stress the verbs, correctly, on the **second** syllable. And if you keep to the original speed you must, again correctly, make the first syllable of each verb very, very short.

You can come in at any point in the book. But there is a logic to the way it is laid out. **Parts 1** and **2** concentrate on the main things that speakers must do in order for other people (native or non-native speakers) to understand them: correct syllable length; linking; weak and strong forms; short and long vowels; rules for placement of stress. **Part 3** looks at what really happens in fast natural speech, so this is where your ears will be trained in order to understand spoken English better (and where you will become aware of how to sound more natural, if that is your aim) **Parts 4** to **6** contain a number of poems to help you practise what has been covered earlier as well as providing a range of vocabulary work.

At the end of the book you will find the completed poems to the various tasks within the text – they are all also on the tape.

Vocabulary work is, in fact, built into the course throughout. And many of the tasks rely on skill in understanding the words as well as the sounds and rhythm. But do not feel that you have to understand every word of a poem before you can start to listen to or repeat it. Before you even look at the vocabulary explanations, just listen to a given poem many, many times. Let the words flow over you. Concentrate not just on the **rhythm** of the language, but also the **music**, the way the words flow up and down (the **intonation**, in fact). When I learn a new language I imagine the sentences swimming by like great fish in the sea. I see them going up and down (and English goes up and down in a great way, in long flowing movements). So listen and listen first. Then take the book and listen again while reading to yourself. Next, listen to short sections, stop the tape and repeat. Listen, stop and repeat. Finally, you will be able to read along with the tape, as if you were swimming along to the rhythm and music of English. Above all, enjoy yourselves. Have fun. That's what it's all about.

Michael Vaughan-Rees
London, 1994.

For my wife, Jane Waller, with love and gratitude.

Part 1

SYLLABLES, STRESS AND RHYTHM

How many syllables?

All words consist of one or more **syllables**. In that first sentence, for example, the words *all*, *words*, *of*, *one*, *or* and *more* just have one syllable, *consist* has two, and *syllables* has three. Listen to the following words. The number of syllables is given at the beginning of each group.

(1) Jane / house / blue / Spain / pears /grow / work / watch / watched / loud / hunt / give

(2) Susan / houses / yellow / Japan/ apples / grower / working / watchful / aloud / hunted / decide / forgive / photo

(3) Timothy / indigo / Germany / bananas / workable / workmanship / watchfulness / decisive / decided / forgiven / tomorrow / cigarette / photograph

(4) Elizabeth / indecisive / Argentina / pomegranates / unforgiven / unworkable / photography / photographic

Task one

Decide how many syllables there are in each of the following words.

biology	( )	bridge	( )	strength	( )	photographer	( )
watches	( )	unabridged	( )	support	( )	jumped	( )
jumpers	( )	policeman	( )	decided	( )	obeyed	( )

The importance of stress

It is important to become aware of the number of syllables in a word. But if you want to speak English with the correct rhythm there is something even more important: the place of **stress**. Listen to the following sequence:

■   ■   ■

Jane, Susan and Timothy.

The first name has one syllable, the second has two and the last has three. But only one syllable in each word is heavily **stressed**. You can see this more clearly if we change the size of the written syllables, according to their relative importance. So, imagine them as:

■   ■ ○   ■ ○ ○

jane, susan and timothy

Stressed syllables, such as jane, su and ti, are different from **unstressed** (sometimes called **weak**) syllables in a number of ways. To start with, they tend to be both relatively **loud** and **long**; relative, that is not only to any other syllables in the same word but also to unimportant words such as *and*.

The importance of stressed syllables in terms of rhythm can be shown if we change the order of the sequence of names. Listen to the following:

■ ■ ■	■ ■ ■
Jane, Susan and Timothy.	Timothy, Susan and Jane.
Susan, Jane and Timothy.	Jane, Timothy and Susan.
Timothy, Jane and Susan.	Susan, Timothy and Jane.

Now repeat each line, keeping to the same rhythm. Clap your hands, click your fingers or tap on the desk to keep to the beat.

■ ■ ■ pause	■ ■ ■ pause
recording	**you**
Jane, Susan and Timothy.	(Jane, Susan and Timothy)
Susan, Jane and Timothy.	(Susan, Jane and Timothy)
Timothy, Jane and Susan.	(Timothy, Jane and Susan)
Timothy, Susan and Jane	(Timothy, Susan and Jane)
Jane, Timothy and Susan.	(Jane, Timothy and Susan)
Susan, Timothy and Jane.	(Susan, Timothy and Jane)

It doesn't matter that the three names have different numbers of syllables. And it doesn't matter in which order they are said. The time between the stressed syllables remains more or less the same, which means that the beat stays the same.
But we can only keep to the ONE TWO THREE beat if we make sure that:

a) the stressed syllable is louder and longer than the others
b) the weak syllables are really weak.

Task two

Here are a number of words taken from different sets: cities in Great Britain; names of boys and girls; animals; countries and rivers. Your first task is to fill in the grid, placing the words according to the number of syllables. The British cities have been done for you as an example:

Ann/elephant/Volga/Felicity/Spain/Wolverhampton/Nile/rhinoceros/
Alexander/Jemima/Japan/Amazon/bear/George/Cardiff/Janet/Peter/
Afghanistan/giraffe/Leith/Mississippi/Anthony/Manchester/Morocco

	1 syllable	2 syllables	3 syllables	4 syllables
Cities	Leith	Cardiff	Manchester	W'hampton
Boys' names				
Girls' names				
Animals				
Countries				
Rivers				

Where is the stress?

Listen to the 2-syllable words from **Task two**.

Janet / Japan / Volga / giraffe / Cardiff / Peter

Each of them has, of course, one **stressed** syllable and one **weak** syllable. But which is which? To put it another way:

Which words have the stress pattern ■ ○ (with the stress on the first syllable)?
And which have the pattern ○ ■ (with the stress on the second) ?

Listen to the words once more. Two words start with a weak syllable; the rest with a strong, stressed syllable. We can again show the difference by changing the size of the letters, thus:

○ ■ giraffe / japan

■ ○ janet / volga / cardiff / peter

Do not be surprised that there are more of one pattern than the other; the vast majority of 2-syllable nouns (names included) have the stress pattern ■ ○. (As we shall see later, most 2-syllable **verbs** are the other way round, having the pattern ○ ■.)

With 3-syllable words there are, of course, three possible patterns:

■ ○ ○ = stress on 1st syllable

○ ■ ○ = stress on 2nd syllable

○ ○ ■ = stress on 3rd syllable

Task three

Listen to the 3-syllable words from the list and place them in the following grid according to their stress pattern.

Manchester / Anthony / Jemima / elephant / Morocco / Amazon

	■ ○ ○	○ ■ ○	○ ○ ■
Manchester			
Anthony			
Jemima			
elephant			
Morocco			
Amazon			

Yes, there was nothing in the third column. In fact there are very few ○ ○ ■ words of any sort. They tend to be either imports such as *cigarette* and *chimpanzee*, or words such as *Japanese* and *picturesque* where the ending is so strong that it becomes the main stress.

Nouns with the ○ ■ ○ pattern are quite rare, too, unless they are derived from verbs (*accountant / allowance / believer / enquiry / excitement*, etc.). And many of them, like *Jemima* and *Morocco*, are imports ending in a vowel letter/sound; think about *banana*, *tobacco*, *spaghetti*, for example.

Task four
Now listen to the 4-syllable words, and fill in the grid as before.

> Felicity / Afghanistan / Alexander / Wolverhampton / rhinoceros /
> Mississippi

Only two stress patterns are given since it is rare for 4-syllable words to be stressed on the first or last syllable.

	○ ■ ○ ○	○ ○ ■ ○
Felicity		
Afghanistan		
Alexander		
Wolverhampton		
rhinoceros		
Mississippi		

Primary and secondary stress

Listen again to the 4-syllable words. In *Alexander*, *Wolverhampton* and *Mississippi*, those with the ○ ○ ■ ○ pattern, the first syllable sounds stronger than the second and fourth, but not as strong as the third. Think of them as:

alexander / wolverhampton / mississippi

A similar thing happens in the case of 3-syllable words with the ○ ○ ■ pattern, e.g.

cigarette / chimpanzee / japanese / picturesque

It is not enough, then, simply to talk of syllables as being either **stressed** or **weak**; with words of three or more syllables it may be necessary to distinguish three degrees of stress:

primary, **secondary** and **weak** (or unstressed).

So, in the case of these two patterns it might be better to show them as:

● ○ ■ (e.g. cigarette) = secondary stress + weak + primary stress, and

● ○ ■ ○ (e.g. Alexander) = secondary stress + weak + primary stress + weak.[1]

Weak syllables and schwa

As a general rule we can say that every syllable contains a vowel sound [2]. A second general rule is that the shorter the vowel, the shorter and weaker the syllable.

Now let us take another look at some of the words already examined, this time concentrating on the vowel sounds in the weak syllables. To help us do this we will start to use phonetic notation, where one symbol = one sound. This is because standard spelling often makes it difficult to see what the sounds really are.

Janet	■ ○	janet	'dʒænɪt / 'dʒænət
Peter	■ ○	peter	'piːtə
giraffe	○ ■	giraffe	dʒə'rɑːf
Japan	○ ■	japan	dʒə'pæn
elephant	■ ○ ○	elephant	'elɪfənt / 'eləfənt
Anthony	■ ○ ○	anthony	'æntəni
Amazon	■ ○ ○	amazon	'æməzən
Morocco	○ ■ ○	morocco	mə'rɒkəʊ
Jemima	○ ■ ○	jemima	dʒɪ'maɪmə / dʒə'maɪmə
cigarette	● ○ ■	cigarette	ˌsɪgə'ret
Felicity	○ ■ ○ ○	felicity	fə'lɪsəti
rhinoceros	○ ■ ○ ○	rhinoceros	rai'nɒsərəs
Wolverhampton	● ○ ■ ○	wolverhampton	ˌwʊlvə'hæmptən
Mississippi	● ○ ■ ○	mississippi	ˌmɪsɪ'sɪpi / ˌmɪsə'sɪpi

If we blow up the phonetic notation it is easy to see which is the most common vowel sound in the weak, unstressed syllables.

Morocco	mə'rɒkəʊ	Amazon	'æməzən
giraffe	dʒə'rɑːf	Peter	'piːtə
Japan	dʒə'pæn	Anthony	'æntəni
Felicity	fə'lɪsəti	rhinoceros	rai'nɒsərəs

---

1 These rules of stress cover words in isolation, in their dictionary form. In Part 2 we will see how stress may shift according to word function.

2 The exception is in words such as *curtain* or *bottle* where /n/ and /l/ may act as 'syllabic consonants', with no need for a preceding short vowel.

cigarette	ˌsɪɡəˈret
Wolverhampton	ˌwʊlvəˈhæmptən
elephant	ˈelɪfənt / ˈeləfənt
Jemima	dʒɪˈmaɪmə / dʒəˈmaɪmə
Janet	ˈdʒænɪt / ˈdʒænət

The most common sound by far is the one in green. This is the vowel represented by the symbol ə; and it is the only vowel important enough to be given its own name: the **schwa**.

The schwa (sometimes spelled **shwa**) is not only the most common vowel sound in weak syllables; it is by far the most common vowel sound in the whole of the English system. Look at its distribution in the words above. It is found:

● at the start of words, just before the main stress;
  e.g. **Mo**rocco, **Ja**pan, **gi**raffe, **Fe**licity

● following main stress (sometimes twice in ■ ○ ○ words);
  e.g. Pe**ter**, A**mazon**, An**tho**ny

● between secondary and primary stress
  e.g. ci**ga**rette, Wol**ver**hampton

● as an even shorter alternative to short /ɪ/ in fast versions of certain words;
  e.g. Ja**net**, Je**mi**ma, e**le**phant

Schwa is not just short; it is the shortest possible vowel in English. Listen to how little difference the presence of schwa can make to a word.

Words without schwa	Words with schwa
sport = spɔːt	support = səˈpɔːt
claps = klæps	collapse = kəˈlæps
prayed = preɪd	parade = pəˈreɪd
scum = skʌm	succumb = səˈkʌm
sliver = ˈslaɪvə	saliva = səˈlaɪvə
train = treɪn	terrain = təˈreɪn
blow = bləʊ	below = bəˈləʊ
cress = kres	caress = kəˈres
plight = plaɪt	polite = pəˈlaɪt
Clyde = klaɪd	collide = kəˈlaɪd
hungry = ˈhʌŋɡri	Hungary = ˈhʌŋɡəri

Note that there is no single written vowel which corresponds to schwa. In the examples just given it is variously found in the syllables <ca->, <ga-> <pa->, <sa->, <be->, <te->, <co-> and <su->. We have already met it in <ja->, <ma->, <je->, <ce->, <ci->, <mo->, and so on.

So there is no point in trying to learn all the possible written forms where the schwa sound can be found. Pay attention instead to the contexts where it is often to be found: the syllables before or after main stress, for example.

Task five

Listen to the following words, all taken from Task one, and circle the syllables containing schwa. (Note, not all words contain schwa.)

grower	yellow	aloud	hunted	forgive	photo
Timothy	Germany	bananas	workmanship	tomorrow	
Elizabeth	Argentina	photograph	photography	photographic	

Stress and rhythm

When we looked at the Jane, Susan and Timothy sequence, we saw that it is possible to keep to a more or less regular beat, based on stressed syllables, provided that:

a) the stressed syllable is louder and longer than the others
b) the weak syllables are really weak.

You can demonstrate this by using the first line of a famous children's rhyme called '**This** is the **house** that **Jack built**'. It has four beats, corresponding to the stressed syllables marked in bold in the previous line. But note that the first beat is followed by two weak syllables, the next by one, then by none. So you have to imagine the rhythm of the line as:

ONE			TWO		THREE	FOUR
■	○	○	■	○	■	■
DAH	du	du	DAH	du	DAH	DAH

This is the house that Jack built

(Note the use of DAH du du DAH du DAH DAH. You can always use these nonsense syllables to get the rhythm of sentences without having to worry about an exact pronunciation. Just remember that DAH is relatively **long and loud**, while **du** is relatively short and quiet.)

Listen to what happens if we keep to the same 4-beat rhythm, while changing the words and varying the number of weak syllables.

ONE			TWO			THREE			FOUR
■	○	○	■	○	○	■	○	○	■
DAH	du	du	DAH	du	du	DAH	du	du	DAH

These are the houses that Jaqueline built

Now try this longer sequence, still keeping to the same rhythm.

ONE	TWO	THREE	FOUR
This is the	house that	Jack	built
These are the	houses that	Jack	built
These are the	houses that	Jaqueline	built
This is the	house that my	mother	designed
This is the	bicycle	Peter	repaired
Those are the	people we	met in the	park
That is the	person I	saw on the	stairs
Those are the	people we	drove to the	party
That is the	gardener who	works for my	mother
Andrew is	taller than	Peter and	Thomas
Fancy a	glass of	Italian	brandy?
Tom's not as	tall as the	rest of the	family
What an	amazingly	lively	production
How can we	possibly	get there in	time!

Schwa in grammatical items

Schwa is found not only in **lexical items** (nouns, main verbs, adjectives and adverbs) . It is regularly found in common, weakly-stressed **grammatical items**, especially prepositions, articles, auxiliary verbs and pronouns.

Task six

Listen again to the house that Jack built sequence and see if you can spot the grammatical items containing schwa.

Strong and weak forms of grammatical items

In Task six we concentrated on weakly stressed grammatical items, all containing schwa. But be careful; do not assume that such items always contain schwa. This can depend on:

● what the item is doing (i.e. its **function**) and/or
● where the item is found (i.e. its **position**).

The word *that*, for example, has two different functions.

1   In 'This is the house **that** Jack built' it is a weakly stressed relative pronoun, with schwa. /ðət/

2   In 'That is the gardener who works for my mother' it is a strongly stressed demonstrative pronoun, with a different, stronger vowel. /ðæt/

The definite article *the* has two different pronunciations according to the following sound.

1   When the next word begins with a consonant (e.g. *the house / the people*) there is the weak form with schwa: ðə ˈhaʊs / ðə ˈpiːpəl

2   but when followed by a vowel (as in *the old man*) it is pronounced /ðiː/, with a /j/ sound linking it to the vowel: /ðiː ʲəʊld mæn/ [3]

The preposition *to* changes according to two criteria of position: the following sound, and its position in the sentence.

1   When followed by a consonant (e.g. *to the party*) the weak form with schwa is used: /tə ðə ˈpɑːti/

2   when followed by a vowel (as in *to a party*) it contains a stronger vowel with a /w/ sound linking it to the vowel: /tu ʷə ˈpɑːti/

3   Finally, if *to* ends a sequence (e.g. *That's where I'm going to*) it is pronounced /tuː/, with an even stronger, longer vowel, as if it were *too* or *two*.

We can say the same about a number of other grammatical items, notably: the **pronouns** *he*, *her*, *him* and *them*; the **possessive adjectives** *her* and *his*; and **modal** and **auxiliary** verbs. These, too, have various **strong** and **weak** forms, and the strongest form of all is used at the end of a sequence, or in contrast with another word.

Take the **pronouns** and **possessive adjectives**. Compare.

strong forms (associated with pointing and/or contrast)

1 **He** is the one who did it!	(ˈhiːˈɪz ðə wʌn ...)
2 I gave it to **him** not **her**!	(... tʊ ˈhɪm nɒt ˈhɜː)
3 It was **them** I saw, over **there**!	(... ˈðem ...)
4 It was **her** fault, not **his**!	(... ˈhɜː ... ˈhɪz)
5 **We** did it, not **you**!	(ˈwiː ... ˈjuː)

very weak forms (usually found after a stressed verb)

1 Where's Peter? I **think** he's over **there**.	(aɪ ˈθɪŋk ɪz)
2 Where's Jane? I've just **left** her on her **own**.	(ˈdʒʌs ˈleft ə rɒn ə ˈrəʊn)
3 Where's John? I've just **left** him on his **own**.	(dʒʌs ˈleft ɪm ɒnɪ ˈzəʊn)
4 Where are your parents? I've just **left** them on their **own**.	(ˈdʒʌs ˈleft əm ɒn ðə ˈrəʊn)
5 She's always **pla**ying her gui**tar**.	(ˈpleɪʲɪŋ əgɪˈtɑː)

---

3   The article *the* also has the form /ðiː/ when heavily stressed, as in the following exchange: 'I had dinner with John Major last week.' '**The** John Major?'

Note that more than one weak form may be possible: for example, *her* can be /hə/, /ɜː/ or /ə/; *them* can be /ðəm/ or /əm/; *you* can be /ju/ or /jə/. Note, too, that the very weak forms of *her*, *him* and *them* can involve not only a weakening of the vowel, but also **elision** of the consonant at the start of the word. This will be looked at in greater detail in Part 3.

Rhythm and linking

In the previous section the word **linking** was used for the first time. So far you have learned that in order to keep to the rhythm you have to hit the stressed syllables and weaken the weak syllables. But there is one more important factor: the rhythm can only flow if words are properly **linked**.

I use the word 'flow' because it can help to think of words as a stream, with no division between them. Or you may prefer to imagine the words as a chain, all joined (or **linked**) together.

There are four main ways of linking words. Here is a simple sequence to help you remember them.

> One apple, two apples, three apples, four apples

In each case the number links smoothly to the following vowel sound, so that the next word sounds as if it doesn't start with a vowel at all. Imagine it like this:

	written as	sounds like	phonetic notation
1	One apple	wu napple	wʌ ˈnæpəl
2	Two apples	two wapples	tuː ʷˈæpəlz
3	Three apples	three yapples	θriː ʲˈæpəlz
4	Four apples	four rapples	fɔː ˈræpəlz

Now let's look at these four types of linking in greater detail.

1 **consonant to vowel** *one apple*
   When a word ending in a consonant is followed by a word beginning with a vowel there is a smooth link. If the word beginning with the vowel is stressed, then the moment of stress seems to begin with the preceding consonant. Compare the following sequences, which sound exactly the same.

   a) What we need is a name.   /əˈneɪm/
   b) What we need is an aim.   /əˈneɪm/

   This is the most common form of linking, and there were several examples in the 'This is the house that Jack built' sequence, including:

> a glass‿of‿Italian brandy
>
> Tom's not‿as tall‿as the rest of the family.
>
> That‿is the person‿I saw on the stairs.

2 rounded vowel to vowel *two apples*

Where a word ends with one of the rounded vowels əʊ, aʊ, u (as in *so, now, too*) there is a /w/ link. For example:

so (h)e's left !	= səʊ ʷiːz 'left
too old	= tuː ʷ'əʊld
Andrew is taller	= 'ændruː ʷɪz 'tɔːlə

This is presumably due to the fact that the lips are coming together anyway, and the consequent parting of the lips in preparation for the next vowel forces a /w/.

3 spread/stretched vowel to vowel *three apples*

Conversely, when a word ends with /iː/ (as in *see, he, she*) or one of the diphthongs of which /ɪ/ is the second element (aɪ, eɪ, ɔɪ, as in *my, they, boy*) there is an off-glide to /j/. For example:

yes, I am	= je saɪʲ 'æm	Fancy a glass?	= 'fænsiʲ ə 'glɑːs
very often	= veriʲ 'ɒfən	my uncle	= maɪʲ 'ʌŋkəl

4 /r/ to vowel *four apples*

In many dialects of English (including General American and several found in Britain) the written <r> in words such as *mother, for,* and *far* has a corresponding /r/ sound. But in RP (and various other 'non-rhotic' dialects) an /r/ sound is only heard when there is a following vowel. Compare the following.

far	= fɑː	far away	= fɑːrə 'wei
for weeks	= fə 'wiːks	for ever	= fə 'revə
mother	= 'mʌðə	mother-in-law	= 'mʌðərɪn lɔː
Peter	= 'piːtə	Peter and Tom	= 'piːtərən 'tɒm

Two other forms of linking

I strongly suggest that you learn to make these four main types of link; it will make your English much smoother, and you will be understood more easily. There are, however, two other types of link which you should know about. Don't feel that you have to imitate them, but you will be able to understand spoken English more easily if you are aware of them.

5 'intrusive' /r/ to vowel

In many words ending with the written consonant <r> the final vowel sound is one of the following: schwa (teacher/ harbour / actor etc.); /ɔː/ (four / door / pour etc.) and /ɑː/ (car / far / bar etc.). No doubt as a result of this, there is a tendency to insert a linking /r/ when a word ends in one of these vowel sounds, even when no written <r> exists. For example:

America and Asia	= ə ˈmerɪkə rə ˈneɪʒə
Asia and America	= ˈeɪʒə rə nə ˈmerɪkə
law and order	= ˌlɔː rə ˈnɔːdə
Shah of Persia	= ʃɑː rəv ˈpɜːʃə / ˈpɜːʒə

Careful with this one. Many people consider that 'intrusive' /r/ is sub-standard, and certainly not to be imitated.

6   consonant to consonant linking

Many words in English start with clusters of two or three consonant sounds. For example, *play / splay / train / strain / dry / try / fly*, and so on.

So when a word ending in a consonant sound is followed by a word beginning with another consonant **with which it can form a cluster**, then there is a tendency for that cluster to occur.

That sounds rather complicated, but is actually a description of what happens with, for example, *cold rain*, where the /d/ is drawn towards the /r/ (since the initial cluster /dr/ is highly productive) so that it sounds like *coal drain*, with the stress starting on /dr/ not on /r/. Other examples include:

actual words	sounds like	phonetic notation
ice cream	I scream	aɪ ˈskriːm
next week	necks tweak	ˌneks ˈtwiːk
six trains	sick strains	ˌsɪk ˈstreɪnz
might rise	my tries	ˌmaɪ ˈtraɪz
Regent's Park	region spark	ˌriːdʒən(t) ˈspɑːk

Billy yate a napple, a nice ri papple

On page 16 there is a chant to help you practise the first three types of linking. The chant is written with the correct spelling on the left of the page, but you actually say it the way it is written on the right.

Vocabulary notes
apples, *oranges* and *apricots* are fruit; *onions*, *artichokes* and *aubergines* are vegetables; *almonds* are nuts; *eels* look like snakes, but live in rivers or the sea; *oysters* are shell-fish which you cut open and eat with a little lemon-juice; *crunchy* here is the opposite of *soft*; *runny* means not cooked for long; you can *smoke* different types of fish, salmon, for example.

How it's written	How it sounds
Billy ate an apple, a nice ripe apple	Billy yate a napple, a nice ri papple
Beattie ate an orange, a nice juicy orange	Beattie yate a norange, a nice juicy yorange
Lucy ate an ice cream, a nice creamy ice cream	Lucy yate a ni scream, a nigh screamy yi scream
Flo ate an apricot, a nice yellow apricot	Flo wate a napricot, a nice yellow wapricot
Mo ate an omelette, a nice runny omelette	Mo wate a nomelette, a nice runny yomelette
Chloe ate an egg, a nice brown egg	Chloe yate a negg, a nice brow negg
Nelly ate an almond, a nice crunchy almond	Nelly yate a nalmond, a nigh scrunchy yalmond
Sally ate an onion, a nice Spanish onion	Sally yate a nonion, a nigh Spani shonion
Alex ate an artichoke, a nice tasty artichoke	Alec sate a nartichoke, a nigh stasty yartichoke
Andrew ate an aubergine, a nice spicy aubergine	Andrew wate a naubergine, a nigh spicy yaubergine
Mary ate an olive a nice Greek olive	Mary yate a nolive, a nigh scree colive
Carol ate an eel, a nice smoked eel	Caro late a neel, a nigh smoke teel
Alice ate an oyster, a nice fresh oyster	Alice sate a noyster, a nice fre shoyster

And what kind of summmer did **you** have?

Here is a chance for you to practise what we've been looking at so far. The poem on pages 17 and 18 has a simple, driving ONE two three ONE two three beat. But you will only keep to the beat if you remember to:

1 hit the main stressed syllables (shown **in bold** in the first three verses);
2 watch out for the weak syllables in the names; a lot of them start with an unstressed syllable containing schwa;
3 watch out also for the weak forms of short grammatical words such as *to*, *and*, *that* and *of*;
4 make the links between words where necessary;

5   and don't be afraid to leave out (**elide**) the occasional sound. We'll be looking at this in greater detail in Part 3, but for the moment just note that *and* often loses its final /d/, especially when followed by a consonant; and *of* may lose its /v/ and just become schwa, also when followed by a consonant. All of these things happen in the second verse, as you can see when it is written in phonetic notation.

■   ■   ■   ■

wɪ ˈdrəʊv θruː ðə ˈnaɪt tʊ ʷə ˈvɪlɪdʒ nɪə ˈbrʌsəlz
tə ˈtʃuːz lɒtsə ˈbuːz ən iː(t) ˈplɛnti ʲə ˈmʌsəlz

Vocabulary notes
booze (*noun/verb*) is slang for '(alcoholic) drink';
to falter is to stop doing something smoothly; talking for instance;
a *Fiesta* is a type of Ford;
gear is a general word for 'things';
a *fee* is money paid for professional services (to a lawyer, architect etc.);
a *loner* is a person who prefers to be alone;
mussels are shell-fish which are very popular in Belgium;
replenish is a formal verb meaning 'fill'.

We **tra**velled to **Ve**nice then on to Ve**ro**na
to **test** a **Fiest**a with **on**ly one **own**er.

We **drove** through the **night** to a **vi**llage near **Bru**ssels
to **choose** lots of **booze** and eat **plen**ty of **mus**sels.

We **la**ter de**ci**ded to **head** off to **Spain**
via **France** for a **chance** to drink **lots** of cham**pagne**.

But after a week of good living and booze
we agreed that we'd need to rest up in Toulouse.

Then we drove to Madrid before heading to Lisbon
to meet our friend Pete who'd just flown in from Brisbane.

We drove farther south to a town near Granada
to find lots of wine to replenish the larder,

and then spent a week just outside Algeciras,
but folk that we spoke to refused to come near us.

We stayed for a while in the town of Pamplona
where Pete walked the street (he's a bit of a loner).

We drove fairly fast to a hotel in Cannes
where we tried to confide our affairs to a man,

who gave us some goods to deliver in Rome
for a fee we'd not see until safely back home.

We sailed down to Malta to stay in Valetta
but a fax sent from Sfax made us think that we'd better,

cross over to Tunis then drive to Algiers
to speak to a Greek I had known for some years.

We drove through Morocco to reach Casablanca
to discuss, without fuss, our affairs with a banker.

Then headed back north, crossed the Straits of Gibraltar
but passed through so fast we were starting to falter,

and round about then I began to remember
I had to meet Dad on the tenth of September.

We sold the Fiesta and loaded a plane
with some gear from Tangier then we got on a train,

which roared through the night till it reached Santander
where we stayed one more day just to breath in the air,

then a boat brought us back to our own native shores.
So that was my holiday, how about yours?

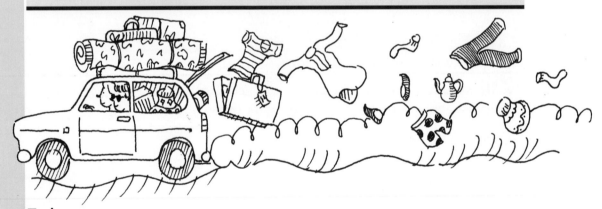

Task seven

Your task is:

a) to write the place names in the table according to their stress pattern (two have been done as examples);

b) to find the **odd one out**; that is to say, the name which follows a pattern not represented in the grid.

■	○■	■○	○■○	●○■○
	Madrid		Valetta	

Rhymes, rhythm and alliteration

The remaining practice poems in Part 1 include one extra element, **alliteration**; that is to say, the repetition of initial consonant sounds.

In the first poem, 'Names', each line contains an English first name, followed by a British place-name, both starting with the same sound, (usually a consonant, but there are two examples of vowels being repeated).

As with the previous poem, – 'What kind of summer did you have?' – this has a simple ONE two three ONE two three waltz beat. But you can only keep to the beat if you remember the following:

1   Several common-place name endings have become so weak that the vowels have been reduced to schwa.

<-ham> = /əm/; Nottingham = ˈnɒtɪŋəm; Birmingham = ˈbɜːmɪŋəm

<-ster> = /stə/; Leicester = ˈlestə; Gloucester = ˈglɒstə

<-ton> = /tən/; Paignton = ˈpeɪntən; Taunton = ˈtɔːntən

<-ford> = /fəd/; Stratford = ˈstrætfəd; Oxford = ˈɒksfəd

2   Most 2-syllable nouns start with a stressed syllable and end with a weaker syllable (often containing schwa). Place names are no exception. But watch out for those which have the main stress on the second syllable.

Dundee   Kildare   Argyll /ɑːˈgaɪəl/   Carlisle /kɑːˈlaɪl/

3   Most 2-syllable first names also start with a stressed syllable. But a number of 3-syllable names (especially ending with <-a>) have the main stress on the second syllable with schwa in the first and third syllables: e.g.

Patricia = pəˈtrɪʃə   Amanda = əˈmændə   Belinda = bəˈlɪndə
Theresa = təˈriːzə or təˈreɪzə

4   The preposition *from* is found in its weak /frəm/ form throughout. But the pronunciation of *and* depends on what the next sound is. The /d/ is only certain to be heard when followed by a vowel (so *and Anne* = ən ˈdæn). But the /d/ is **elided** in, for example, *and Stan* and we hear /ən ˈstæn/.

5   But sometimes when the /d/ disappears it allows **assimilation** to take place. This means that a sound changes to be more like the following sound. In *and Patricia*, for example the /d/ goes and then the /n/ becomes /m/ because of the following /p/ and we end up with əm pəˈtrɪʃə. In the same way, *and Kate* = əŋ ˈkeɪt.(The symbol /ŋ/ represents the consonant sound at the end of *song*, *thing*, *wrong* etc.).

(Don't worry if this is not very clear at the moment. We will look at elision and assimilation in more detail in Part 3.)

6   And careful with the links in, for example, *and Anne*; *Chester and*; *Joyce is*; *from Argyll*; etc.

Names

1 **Nor**man's from **Not**tingham,
  Martin's from **Mot**tingham,
  Charley's from **Ches**ter
  and **Les**ley's from **Lee**;
  Joyce is from **Jar**row
  and **Hen**ry's from **Har**row,
  Laura's from **Leic**ester
  and **Dave's** from Dun**dee**.

2 **Ted** comes from **Taun**ton
  and **Stan** comes from **Staun**ton
  Billy's from **Bol**ton
  And **Wil**ly's from **Ware**;
  Mary's from **Mar**low,
  and **Har**ry's from **Har**low
  Mike's from South **Mol**ton
  and **Kate's** from Kil**dare**.

3 **Step**hen's from **Strat**ford
  and **Cuth**bert's from **Cat**ford,
  Stanley's from **Stain**ton
  and **Cor**a's from **Cork**;
  Graham's from **Goole**
  and Pa**tric**ia's from **Poole**,
  Patrick's from **Paign**ton,
  Yolan**da**'s from **York**.

4 **Ken's** from Car**lisle**
  and **Anne's** from Ar**gyll**,
  Fanny's from **Faw**ley
  and **Har**riet's from **Hull**;
  Teddy's from **Ten**by
  and **Den** is from **Den**bigh,
  Chris comes from **Craw**ley
  and **Mil**lie's from **Mull**.

5 **Ed** comes from **Elt**ham
  and **Fred** comes from **Felt**ham,
  Brian's from **Brain**tree
  and **Chris** comes from **Crewe**;
  Colin's from **Ker**ry
  and **Bob**by's from **Bur**y,
  Ada's from **Ain**tree
  So, **how** about **you**?

Where do you think you're going?

This is another poem in 3/4 time. The beat is strictly as follows:

and	ONE	2	3	ONE	2	3	ONE	2	3	ONE	2	(and)
du	DAH	du	du	DAH	du	du	DAH	du	du	DAH	du	

I'm going to Leeds to locate a libretto
I'm going to Stockholm to steal a stiletto

It is important to remember the following:

1 The place names are either monosyllables (*Leeds, Slough, Cork, Cowes*, etc.) or have the stress pattern ■ ○, as is normal for 2-syllable nouns (*Brighton, Ventnor, Poland*, etc.).

2 The verbs are either monosyllables (*buy, view, sell, pinch*, etc.) or have the stress pattern ○ ■, as is normal for 2-syllable verbs (*provide, supply, collect, locate, promote, consult, reform, confuse, become*).

3   All the 3-syllable nouns at the end of lines have the pattern ○ ■ ○. This is either because they derive from ○ ■ verbs (*professor, confessor, relation, computer, commuter*) or because they are loan words from other languages all ending in a vowel sound (*banana, pyjama, vanilla, confetti, spaghetti, libretto, stiletto, baloney*).

4   The two loan words with four syllables (*sarsparilla* and *macaroni*) have the pattern ● ○ ■ ○, i.e. there is secondary stress on the first syllable and primary stress on the third.

5   If the place has only one syllable (*Leeds, Perth, Cork* etc.) then the verb has two syllables, (*provide, supply, collect*). But if the place has two syllables, (*Stockholm, Soho, Poland, Basel*) then the verb has one (*buy, steal, pinch*).

Vocabulary notes

baloney is a type of sausage (from Bologna in Italy);
a *commuter* lives in the suburbs and travels (or commutes) into the city to work;
confetti are bits of coloured paper thrown over the couple after a wedding;
a *libretto* is the words of an opera;
pastrami is a type of smoked beef (US);
pinch is a colloquial word for steal;
sarsparilla is a soft drink made from the sarsparilla plant;
a *steeple* is the tower of a church;
a *stiletto* is a sharp, pointed knife;
vanilla comes from a type of bean and is used for flavouring desserts.

Where do you think you're going?

I'm going to Brighton to buy some bananas
I'm going to Perth to provide some pyjamas

I'm going to Ventnor to view some vanilla
I'm going to Slough to supply sarsparilla

I'm going to Soho to sell some salami
I'm going to Poland to pinch some pastrami

I'm going to Cork to collect some confetti
I'm going to Spain to secure some spaghetti

I'm going to Leeds to locate a libretto
I'm going to Stockholm to steal a stiletto

I'm going to Prague to promote my professor
I'm going to Crewe to consult my confessor

I'm going to Rye to reform a relation
I'm going to Stansted to stare at the station

> I'm going to Basel to boil some baloney
> I'm going to Minsk for some mixed macaroni
>
> I'm going to Plymouth to please all the people
> I'm going to Stockport to stand on the steeple
>
> I'm going to Cowes to confuse a computer
> I'm moving to Kent to become a commuter

Now listen to the poem very carefully and answer the following questions.

Task eight
Which of the 2-syllable place names have schwa in the final syllable? Which may have schwa? And which definitely do not have schwa?

Task nine
Which of the final words in each line have schwa in the first syllable?

Task ten
Which of the final words also have schwa in the last syllable?

Task eleven
Which of the verbs have schwa in the first syllable?

The do-it-yourself tongue-twister kit

Every language has what are called **tongue-twisters**: sequences with so many examples of alliteration that even native speakers have problems saying them fast. (Examples in English include: *Peter Piper picked a peck of pickled pepper* and *She sells sea-shells on the sea-shore*.)

In 'Names' there were just **two** examples of each consonant sound; *Martin's from Mottingham*, for example. In 'Where do you think you're going?' it went up to **three**; *I'm going to Brighton to buy some bananas*, and so on. In this section we will end up with **five** or sometimes **six**. But we'll make it easier for you by starting with just two examples of the same sound, then building up to three, four, and so on. (It's called 'The do-it-yourself tongue-twister kit' because you start off easy and take your time working up to the more difficult ones.)

two-part alliteration
The most important syllables in this part are found in the **name** and in what the person **buys** to eat or drink. The word *bought* is more important than the very weak *some* (= /səm/) , but it is less important than the main syllables, because it is repeated. Watch out for the words (including names) with stress on the second syllables:

poˈtatoes, baˈnanas, toˈmatoes, saˈlome, caˈmilla, paˈtricia.

They all have schwa in the first weak syllable!

Vocabulary notes
cabbages and *potatoes* are vegetables; *peaches* and *bananas* are fruit; *doughnuts*, *chocolate* and *fritters* contain sugar; *cod* is a fish, and *salami* is a type of sausage.

■	●	■
Kenneth	bought some	**cabb**age.
Polly	bought some	**peach**es.
Sally	bought some	**sa**lad.
Dennis	bought some	**dough**nuts.
Charles	bought some	**choc**olate.
Shirley	bought some	**su**gar.
Freddy	bought some	**frit**ters.
Camilla	bought some	**cod**.
Tina	bought some	**to**matoes.
Barbara	bought some	**bana**nas.
Salome	bought some	**sa**lami.
Patricia	bought some	**po**tatoes.

three-part alliteration

Now we add another word to say how much food or drink is bought. This can be a **container** (*a packet, tin, crate*, etc.); a **quantity** (*a dozen, slice, pound, kilo*, etc.); or we can add *-ful* to some of the nouns. The main syllable in the new word is stressed, but the linking word *of* is very, very weak. When followed by a **vowel** we usually pronounce it /əv/ but when followed by a **consonant** it often reduces to schwa. This means that *a kilo of cabbage* sounds like *a kilo a cabbage* and *a bunch of bananas* sounds like *a bunch a bananas*.

■	●	■	■
Kenneth	bought a	**ki**lo of	**cabb**age.
Polly	bought a	**pack**et of	**peach**es.
Sally	bought a	**sack**ful of	**sa**lad.
Dennis	bought a	**do**zen	**dough**nuts.
Charles	bought a	**chunk** of	**choc**olate.
Shirley	bought a	**shop**ful of	**su**gar.
Freddy	bought a	**fridge**ful of	**frit**ters.
Camilla	bought a	**crate** of	**cod.**
Tina	bought a	**tin** of	**to**matoes.
Barbara	bought a	**bunch** of	**bana**nas.
Salome	bought a	**slice** of	**sa**lami.
Patricia	bought a	**pound** of	**po**tatoes.

Arthur bought an armful of artichokes

Let's practice this three-part alliteration with the following poem. You will get the rhythm if you pause very slightly after *bought* in each line. Careful, though; the following lines contain **four** examples of the same initial sound:

> **Jer**emy bought a **gi**ant **jar** of **jam**,
> **L**inda bought a **large leg** of **lamb**.
> **Char**lie bought a **chunk** of **cheap cheese**.

To keep to the rhythm in these lines you have to be careful to reduce the word *of* to a simple schwa and link it to the word before it. It has to sound like *a gian(t) jar a jam / a large leg a lamb / a chunk a cheap cheese*.

Vocabulary notes

Important! Don't feel you have to understand every single word before you start listening to the poems. Concentrate on the rhythm and intonation ; listen and start repeating; **then** check the meaning, if you need to.

Artichokes, *beans*, *peas* and *spinach* are vegetables; *apricots*, *lemons* and *quinces* are fruit; *bream* and *sardines* are fish; *lamb*, *mince* and *steak* refer to meat (*mince* is the meat in hamburgers); a *chunk* is a square piece; *doughnuts* are a type of bun cooked in deep fat and covered with sugar; *muesli* is a breakfast cereal; a *mug* is like a cup, but shaped like a cylinder; a *stone* is 14 pounds, about 6 kilos; *toffee* is made with sugar; *thread* is used for sewing clothes, and when you are sewing you put a *thimble* on your finger to push the needle through.

Arthur bought (pause) an **arm**ful of **ar**tichokes,
Belinda bought (pause) a **bar**relful of **beans**,
Catherine bought (pause) a **ki**lo of **ca**bbages, and
Sandra bought (pause) a **sack** of sar**dine**s.

Harriet bought a **hand**ful of **hand**kerchiefs,
Jeremy bought a **gi**ant **jar** of **jam**,
Lola bought a **lit**re of **lem**on juice, and
Linda bought a **large leg** of **lamb**.

Peter bought a **pock**etful of **pea**nuts,
Queenie bought a **quar**ter pound **quince**,
Shirley bought a **shop** full of **su**gar lumps, and
Michael bought a **mi**lligram of **mince**.

Salome bought a **slice** of salami,
Charlie bought a **chunk** of **cheap cheese**,
Spencer bought a **spoon**ful of **spin**ach, and
Pamela bought a **pa**cket full of **peas**.

Philippa bought a **fol**der for her **pho**tographs,
Stephen bought a **stone** of **steak**.
Amos bought an **a**cre of **a**pricots, and
Katie bought a **ki**logram of **cake**,

Cuthbert bought a **cup**ful of **cus**tard,
Brenda bought a **bu**cketful of **bream**,
Ma**til**da bought a **mug**ful of **mus**tard, and
Christopher bought a **crate**ful of **cream**.

Kenneth bought a **car**ton of **co**ffee,
Benedict bought a **bas**ket full of **bread**,
Tina bought a **tin**ful of **to**ffee, and
Theo bought a **thim**ble full of **thread**.

Brian bought some **bread** for his **bro**ther,
David bought some **dough**nuts for his **Dad**,
Muriel made some **mu**esli for her **mo**ther
But **Ma**ry had no **mo**ney and she **just felt sad**.

four-part alliteration

Now we drop the word *bought* and put in its place another alliterative word. This will give it a ONE two three ONE two three beat. Careful with the verbs se**lect**, co**llect**, and de**liv**er, with stress on the second syllable and schwa in the first.

> ### Vocabulary notes
> *purchase*, *select* and *seek* (past = *sought*) are relatively formal verbs; their less formal equivalents are *buy*, *choose* (or *pick*) and *look for* ; to *shift* = 'move from one place to another'; and *a dozen* = 12.

■	■	■	■
Kenneth	col**lec**ted a	**ki**lo of	**cabb**age.
Polly	**pur**chased a	**pack**et of	**peach**es.
Sally	**sought** a	**sack**ful of	**sa**lad.
Dennis	de**liv**ered a	**do**zen	**dough**nuts.
Charles	**chewed** a	**chunk** of	**choc**olate.
Shirley	**shif**ted a	**shop**ful of	**su**gar.
Freddy	**fried** a	**fridge**ful of	**fritt**ers.
Tina	**tas**ted a	**tin** of	to**ma**toes.
Sa**lo**me	se**lec**ted a	**slice** of	sa**la**mi.
Pa**tri**cia	**picked** a	**pound** of	po**ta**toes.

Artful Arthur

This is the final part of 'The do-it-yourself tongue-twister' sequence. Of course each noun, adjective and verb is stressed. But to do this as a rhythmic chant there have to be four main beats (indicated in bold in the first few lines). Most of the lines have the following rhythm:

ONE   TWO   THREE   and   FOUR   and   FIVE   and
■   ●   ■   ■   ■

Artful Arthu**r ar**gued for a**n arm**ful o**f art**ichokes.

And remember to link the words where necessary. You should be doing it automatically by now. So say:

Artful Arthu**r ar**gued for a**n arm**ful o**f art**ichokes.
= ˈɑːtfə ˈlɑːθə ˈrɑːɡjuːd fərə ˈnɑːmfələ ˈvɑːtɪtʃəʊks

Because the vocabulary is fairly difficult you will have to use a dictionary quite a lot in order to understand it. So we end up with two matching tasks to help you remember the meanings of most of the verbs and adjectives.

> **Vocabulary notes**
> These notes are just for the nouns; *cardamom*, *fenugreek* and *vanilla* are all used for flavouring food; *gazpacho* is a Spanish summer soup, made with tomatoes and cucumber; *nougat* is a type of sweet, or candy, from France; *clams* are shell-fish; a *sliver* is a very thin slice; *sturgeon* and *tuna* are fish; *treacle* comes from sugar.

ONE   TWO   THREE   and   FOUR   and   FIVE   and
■   ●   ■   ■   ■

Artful Arthu**r ar**gued for a**n arm**ful o**f art**ichokes.
Able Amo**s ached** for an **a**cre o**f a**pricots.
Barmy Barbara **bar**gained for a **ba**sket of ba**na**nas.
Beautiful Belin**da** boiled a **bar**relful of **beans**.
Brash Brenda **bran**dished a **brief**-case full of **bran**.
Careful Catherine **cooked** a **ki**lo of **cabb**ages.
Carmen calmly **car**ted off a **cart**load of **car**damom.
Cheerful Charlie **chose** a **chew**y chunk of **choc**olate.
Clever Chloe **clung** to a **clus**ter of **clams**.
Dirty Duncan **dreamed** of a **doz**en dainty **duck**-eggs.
Fragrant Freda fried a fridge full of fritters.
Furtive Freddy fondled a fistful of fenugreek.
Gorgeous Gertrude gasped for a gallon of gazpacho.
Greedy Grenville grasped for a gross of green grapefruit.
Happy Harry hauled away a hamper full of ham.
Jerky Gerald juggled with some jars of jam.
Lazy Lawrence lugged away a lorry-load of lettuce.
Little Lola lapped up a litre of lemon juice.

Merry Michael munched a milligram of mince.
Naughty Norma gnawed a knob of nutty nougat.
Posh Patricia purchased a pound of Polish peaches.
Queasy Quentin quaffed a quarter-pint of quince-juice.
Sad Sally savoured a sack full of sandwiches.
Sheepish Shirley shattered a shop full of shell-fish.
Sly Salome sliced off a sliver of salami.
Spotty Spencer spattered a spoonful of spinach.
Stocky Stephen stood on a stone of sticky sturgeon.
Tiny Tina tasted a teaspoonful of tuna.
Tricky Trevor traded a trunkful of treacle.
Vicious Victor vanished in a van full of vanilla.
Weary Wanda waded in a waggon load of water-cress.

Task twelve

Match the adjectives with their definitions or synonyms.

1	artful	**a)**	having a bad skin condition
2	able	**b)**	nice-smelling, perfumed
3	barmy	**c)**	really small
4	brash	**d)**	happy (possibly because of the effect of alcohol)
5	cheerful	**e)**	clever, full of tricks, cunning, sly
6	fragrant	**f)**	uncontrolled in one's movements, clumsy
7	furtive	**g)**	misbehaved, or possibly slightly improper
8	gorgeous	**h)**	happy, in a good mood
9	greedy	**i)**	capable, skilful, clever
10	jerky	**j)**	always wanting more things, especially to eat
11	merry	**k)**	really beautiful
12	naughty	**l)**	over-confident, loud, too full of oneself
13	posh	**m)**	mad, crazy, not all there
14	queasy	**n)**	dishonestly tricky, unwilling to confide in others
15	sad	**o)**	quite short, but well-built
16	sly	**p)**	feeling slightly sick, uneasy about a possible action
17	spotty	**q)**	deceitful, clever in cheating, difficult to handle.
18	stocky	**r)**	sly, not wanting to be seen, up to no good
19	tiny	**s)**	upper-class, over-conscious of one's importance
20	tricky	**t)**	unhappy, down in the dumps, miserable

Task thirteen

Match the verbs with their definitions or synonyms.

1 ache	**a)** to transport
2 argue	**b)** to breath in suddenly and loudly
3 bargain	**c)** to cut a thin section from a loaf of bread, a cake, etc.
4 boil	**d)** to grab and hold on to with one or both hands
5 brandish	**e)** to wave in the air
6 cling	**f)** to cook in water at 100 degrees Celsius
7 fry	**g)** to hurt, be in pain, long for
8 fondle	**h)** to bite steadily at something till it is worn away
9 gasp	**i)** to drink steadily (old–fashioned)
10 grasp	**j)** to try to get something for a lower price
11 haul	**k)** to drink the way a cat does
12 juggle	**l)** to eat or taste while enjoying the flavour
13 lug	**m)** to hold tightly to something with both arms
14 lap	**n)** to throw liquid or semi–liquid matter on to something
15 munch	**o)** to move or transport with difficulty
16 gnaw	**p)** to dispute, quarrel, disagree verbally
17 purchase	**q)** to keep three or more objects in the air simultaneously
18 quaff	**r)** to walk in liquid which comes up higher than the ankles
19 savour	**s)** to stroke gently and affectionately
20 shatter	**t)** to chew carefully and steadily, while making some noise
21 slice	**u)** to disappear
22 spatter	**v)** to break something fragile into many small pieces
23 vanish	**w)** to cook in oil or fat
24 wade	**x)** to buy

Part 2

PART 2

STRESS IN WORDS AND PHRASES

In Part 1 the following points were made about stress:

- In words of two or more syllables, one syllable is more important than the other(s). If all the other syllables are weak then we can call this the **stressed syllable**.

- In words of three or more syllables we may have to distinguish three degrees of stress, however. The most important syllable will carry **primary stress**; the next in importance will carry **secondary stress**; the rest can be called **weak**.

- The weakest possible syllables contain the schwa vowel, the shortest and most common vowel sound in English.

- Grammatical items are usually weak, many of them containing schwa (though some may also have a strong form).

- Certain word stress patterns are more common than others. Two-syllable verbs, for example, usually have the pattern ○ ■. Two-syllable nouns, by contrast, usually have the opposite pattern: ■ ○.

In this part we will look in more detail at the rules for stress, both in words and in phrases. And we will see exactly when certain rules can be broken.

A Stress in verbs

Task fourteen

In this section we will consider seven different stress patterns for verbs. But before you read what the rules are, carry out the following task.

- Read and listen to the verbs in the list below.

- Look at the grids, where you will find an example of the seven stress patterns.

- Place each verb in its correct place. (Two have already been put in as examples.)

Some patterns are easier to see (and hear) than others. But the purpose of this task is for you to discover if there are any which cause you problems. **Those** are the ones that you will need to concentrate on. (Note that the numbers 1 to 7 correspond to the different sub-sections in this main section.)

clarify	pre-set	prefer	accelerate	contradict
wander	soften	enliven	refuse	sentimentalise
interfere	defuse	apologise	damage	collect
abolish	co-chair	identify	occupy	measure
undertake	circularise	defend	prepaint	consider
substitute	surrender	overwhelm	monopolise	determine
remove	demist	understand	worry	idolise

1 surprise	2 develop	3 reload	4 introduce
collect			contradict

5 tremble	6 estimate	7 realise

A1 2-syllable verbs ○ ■

Most 2-syllable verbs, as we have seen, start with a weakly stressed syllable. Here are the most common of these initial syllables, together with a selection of the verbs containing them. They are grouped by vowel.

those containing schwa
<a-> <ab-> <co-> <com-> <con-> <for-> <o-> <ob-> <per-> <po-> <pro-> <su-> <sur-> <sus->

abridge / absorb / abuse / account / accuse / allow / amuse / announce / avert / avoid / collapse / collect / collide / command / compare / compete / compose / conduct / confide / conserve / ferment / forget / forgive / object / observe / obstruct / offend / persuade / pervert / police / pollute / produce / protect / subside / subject / subvert / suffice / suggest / surprise / survey / suspect / sustain

those containing short /ɪ/
<en-> <ig-> <im-> <in->

endure / enforce / engage / ignite / ignore / implode /
imply / import / impute / incline / increase / infect /
include / invite

those containing short /ɪ/, though schwa is an alternative
<be-> <de-> <dis-> <e-> <pre-> <re-> <se->

become / behave / believe / bereave / beseech / debate /
decide / defect / defy / deny / derive / devote / distract /
elate / endure / enquire / equip / escape / escort / prefer /
prepare / present / presume / rebel / record / recite / regret /
rehearse / remove / refer / restore / secrete / secure /
sedate / seduce

Note: this group includes a fairly large category of verbs (convict / contrast /
decrease / ferment / record / import / increase / incline /
rebel / pervert / object / subject / suspect / survey etc.) where the
corresponding nouns have the opposite stress pattern: ■ ○. See B1.

A2 3-syllable verbs ○ ■ ○

There are fewer ○ ■ ○ than ○ ■ verbs. Most start with one of the weak initial
syllables you have just met: e.g.

abolish / accomplish / admonish / assemble / awaken /
bewilder / consider / continue / determine / develop / dissemble /
encourage / endanger / enliven / envisage / resemble / surrender

Note that most of these verbs end with a syllable that is normally weak: <-er>, <-en>,
<-ish>, <-age>, <-it>. More about final syllables in A5 on page 35.

Task fifteen
On the tape there is a series of sentences, each containing one of the verbs you have
just met. There is no rhyme this time, but each sentence has the same beat, with a
strong syllable followed by two weak ones.

ONE 2 3 ONE 2 3 ONE 2 3 ONE 2 (and)
DAH du du DAH du du DAH du du DAH du (and)
Conrad composed a concerto for trumpet
Annie announced she had written a novel

You can only keep to the beat if you remember that each of the verbs starts with a really weak syllable. But it's time to mention one more thing about the stressed syllables: they are not just louder and longer than the weak ones; they are usually different in **pitch**. That is to say, that they are often higher or lower than the surrounding unstressed syllables. Not only that: a stressed syllable can change pitch, can go down or up smoothly.

Before you repeat the various poems, chants, raps, and so on, in this book you should do two things: listen to the **rhythm** of course, make sure you hit the stresses and shorten the weak syllables; but you also have to listen to the **music** of the language, to the intonation (i.e. the way the voice goes up and down). So the sentence we have just looked at can be thought of as:

Conrad composed a concerto for trumpet.

if we only think of the rhythm. But we must not forget that it may also sound like:

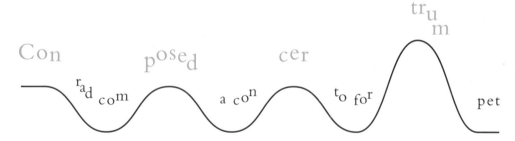

Now you have a choice. You can just listen to the sentences and repeat them. But, if you want to do some vocabulary practice first, try to match the beginnings and endings of the sentences, **then** listen to the recording.

And when you repeat the sentences, do not be fooled by the spelling of name and verb at the start of each sentence. Pairs such as *Percy/persuade* and *Connie/conduct* may look as if they contain the same vowel sound. Listen carefully, however. Each name starts with a stressed syllable, so the vowel sound in the name is always stronger than the weak vowel sound in the first syllable of the verb! Thus *Connie* = ˈkɒniː, whereas *conduct* = kənˈdʌkt.

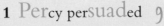

1 Percy persuaded **g**	a) a vaccine for polio
2 Colin collected **p**	b) a symphony orchestra
3 Dennis developed **a**	c) she had written a novel
4 Reggie restored **e**	d) to start up a business
5 Betty became **j**	e) all the frescos in Florence
6 Oscar objected **k**	f) a major catastrophe
7 Benny behaved **m**	g) the troops to surrender
8 Avril averted **f**	h) a classical record
9 Annie announced **c**	i) all the men who'd betrayed him
10 Esther escaped **n**	j) a quite famous celebrity
11 Desmond devoted **o**	k) when others accepted
12 Rita recorded **h**	l) a peaceful solution
13 Forster forgave **i**	m) in a confident manner
14 Connie conducted **b**	n) from a prisoner of war camp
15 Debbie decided **d**	o) his life to the people
16 Susie suggested **l**	p) some marvellous furniture

A3 ● ■ (○) verbs with a true prefix as first syllable

In most ○ ■ and ○ ■ ○ verbs, the weak initial syllable comes from a preposition in Latin. In English the original meaning is often hidden. The fact that <sub->, for example, originally meant 'under' is not clear in such words as *submit* or *subject* (though it is clearer in words such as *sub-section* or *submarine*).

In some verbs, by contrast, the original meaning is still very clear. In such cases we can describe the first syllable as a true **prefix**. (The weaker equivalents may be thought of as 'semi-prefixes'.) True prefixes have strong vowels and will be transcribed showing **secondary** stress within the word. For example:

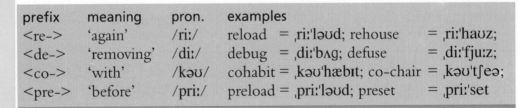

prefix	meaning	pron.	examples
<re->	'again'	/riː/	reload = ˌriːˈləʊd; rehouse = ˌriːˈhaʊz;
<de->	'removing'	/diː/	debug = ˌdiːˈbʌg; defuse = ˌdiːˈfjuːz;
<co->	'with'	/kəʊ/	cohabit = ˌkəʊˈhæbɪt; co-chair = ˌkəʊˈtʃeə;
<pre->	'before'	/priː/	preload = ˌpriːˈləʊd; preset = ˌpriːˈset

But be careful. Each of the above four has a weaker version, where the original meaning is less clear. Look at the examples at the top of the next page.

with prefix		with 'semi-prefix'	
repaint	= ˌriː'peɪnt	remove	= rɪ'muːv or rə'muːv
reset	= ˌriː'set	reject	= rɪ'dʒekt or rə'dʒekt
reform	= ˌriː'fɔːm	reform	= rɪ'fɔːm or rə'fɔːm
	(=form again)		(= improve, rectify)
demist	= ˌdiː'mɪst	deceive	= dɪsiːv or də'siːv
deselect	= ˌdiːsə'lekt	defend	= dɪ'fend or də'fend
co–exist	= ˌkəʊɪg'zɪst	collide	= kə'laɪd
co–chair	= ˌkəʊ'tʃeə	command	= kə'mɑːnd
pre–pay	= ˌpriː'peɪ	prepare	= prɪ'peə or prə'peə
pre–paint	= ˌpriː'peɪnt	prefer	= prɪ'fɜː or prə'fɜː

Note that negative prefixes, such as <un->, <mis-> and <dis->, may also carry secondary stress within the word. e.g. unburden / unsettle / discourage / disfigure / discredit / mismanage, and so on.

A4 3-syllable verbs ● ○ ■

In these verbs the primary stress is on the third syllable and the middle syllable is very weak (usually containing schwa). But there is a noticeable secondary stress on the first syllable. This happens for one of three reasons:

a) The verb starts with a two-syllable prefix, e.g.

ˌintro'duce / ˌinter'vene / ˌcontra'dict / ˌcontra'vene / ˌunder'take / ˌover'whelm / ˌunder'stand / ˌinter'fere

b) A prefix is added to a regular ○ ■ verb, e.g.

ˌdisa'ppoint / ˌreab'sorb / ˌdisa'llow / ˌreco'mmend

c) There are two monosyllabic prefixes, e.g.

ˌcoin'cide / ˌappre'hend / ˌcompre'hend

A5 ■ ○ verbs

If a verb has this pattern it is due to the presence of a final syllable which is always weak, causing the previous syllable to be stressed.

This rule applies whatever the number of syllables and over-rides the general rule that 2-syllable words tend to have the ○ ■ pattern. On the next page are the most common of these weak final syllables, together with their pronunciation and a selection of words containing them.

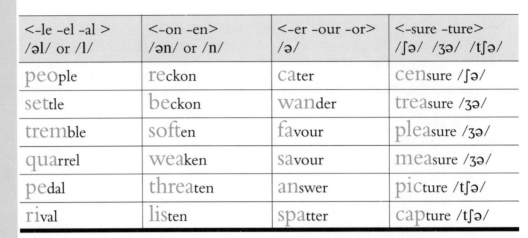

<-le -el -al > /əl/ or /l/	<-on -en> /ən/ or /n/	<-er -our -or> /ə/	<-sure –ture> /ʃə/ /ʒə/ /tʃə/
people	reckon	cater	censure /ʃə/
settle	beckon	wander	treasure /ʒə/
tremble	soften	favour	pleasure /ʒə/
quarrel	weaken	savour	measure /ʒə/
pedal	threaten	answer	picture /tʃə/
rival	listen	spatter	capture /tʃə/

<-ow> /əʊ/	<-age> /ɪdʒ/	<-ish> /ɪʃ/	<-it> /ɪt/	<-y> /i/
follow	damage	vanish	edit	envy
hollow	manage	banish	posit	tidy
borrow	ravage	finish	debit	worry
pillow	savage	nourish	credit	scurry
mellow	pillage	flourish	limit	query
		relish	profit	chivvy

A number of comments have to be made about verbs with these endings, however.

● In many cases (*people, pedal, credit, query, savage, finish, hollow, favour, treasure*, etc.) these verbs can also function as nouns. This particular stress rule applies whatever the class of word.

● You have to be careful about word endings. The letters <-er> may well end a word without being a suffix. In ○ ■ verbs such as deter, inter, refer, confer and defer, for example, it is the elements <ter> and <fer> which are units, not <-er>.

● Careful with <-jure>, too. In words such as abjure, injure, perjure, conjure (= 'do tricks' – pronounced ˈkʌndʒə), conjure (= 'ask solemnly' – pronounced ˌkənˈdʒʊə) the <jure> element forms the unit. Confusion with the regular <ure> ending seems to be the cause of the inconsistency in pronunciation.

● And not all verbs ending in <-it> have a final weak syllable. A number including permit, omit, transmit, remit and submit are standard ○ ■ verbs, since the <mit> element is the unit (e.g. <mission> in the noun derivants).

● Most established words in <-age> have the short /ɪdʒ/ ending. This is also the pronunciation of <-age> as a suffix (in, for instance, *seepage, footage, shrinkage* etc.). But more recent borrowings from French (arbitrage / triage / corsage /

camouflage etc.) tend to end in the much longer /ɑːʒ/. And *garage* varies between the two, being pronounced in a variety of ways, including: 'gærɑːʒ, 'gærɑːdʒ, 'gærɪdʒ, gə'rɑːʒ and gə'rɑːdʒ.

● Finally, careful with allow

A6 (○) ■ ○ ○ *verbs*

Some suffixes cause the main stress to fall on the syllable two from the end (the 'ante-penultimate'). This happens however many syllables come before the stress.

<-ate> /eɪt/ [1]	<-ute> /juːt/ or /tʃuːt/	<-ify> /ɪfaɪ/	<-iply> <-upy> /ɪplaɪ/ /ʊpaɪ/
congregate	institute	dignify	multiply
estimate	constitute	clarify	Occupy
fascinate	substitute	amplify	
assimilate	prostitute	fortify	
accelerate		identify	
negotiate		personify	

A7 *verbs derived from nouns or adjectives by means of the suffix /aɪz/*

A large number of verbs are derived from nouns and adjectives by means of this suffix, variously spelled <-ise>, <ize>. The verbs keep the main stress of the original word. Examples include:

original word →	derived verb	original word →	derived verb
sympathy	sympathise/ize	circular	circularise/ize
Idol	Idolise/ize	real	realise
critic	criticise/ize	organ	Organise
capital	capitalise/ize	character	characterise/ize
apology	apologise/ize	sentimental	sentimentalise
institutional	institutionalise	monopoly	monopolise/ize

---

1 The <-ate> ending is often much weaker in nouns and adjectives. Thus *estimate* as a noun, and *approximate* as an adjective both end /ət/.

B Stress in nouns and adjectives

Task sixteen

Task fourteen in section A made you think about the different stress patterns in verbs. Now we will do the same for nouns. Your task is to:

● Listen to and read the poem: 'Who's who?'. (As you can see, it is full of nouns with a variety of different syllables and stress patterns. But if you keep to the 3/4 beat you will have no choice but to hit the main stressed syllables correctly.)

● Pay special attention to the nouns listed below.

● Place the nouns in the grid – where possible – according to their stress patterns. But note carefully! In Task fourteen you had to find five verbs for each pattern. This time, however, you do not know how many words will go in each column. And also there are some odd ones out; i.e. some nouns which do not belong with the others in the grid!

poet	neurotic	tailor	zoologist	selector
once	teacher	airman	cosmonaut	realist
diver	royalist	hack	geographer	philanthropist
confessor	doctor	wrestler	translator	astronaut
loyalist	barrister	idealist	photographer	broker
physician	balloonist			

a) healer	b) chairman	c) democrat	d) musician

e) technologist	f) loyalist	g) psychotic

Who's who?

When you repeat this poem do not assume that syllables which are spelled the same are always pronounced the same. In Task fifteen , if you recall, you met various pairs of words including:

Percy / **per**suaded   **Col**in / **col**lected
Dennis / **de**veloped   **Av**ril / **av**erted

In each case the name contained a strong, stressed vowel, while the unstressed semi-prefix in the verb was considerably weaker.

There is a similar contrast in 'Who's Who?', this time between the vowel sounds in pairs of nouns and names. For example:

Col's a **col**lector	**Di**'s a **di**rector
ˈkɒlz ə kəˈlektə	ˈdaɪzə dəˈrektə
Con's a **con**fessor	**Sol**'s a **sol**icitor
ˈkɒnz ə kənˈfesə	ˈsɒlz ə səˈlɪsɪtə

The reason is quite clear; all the nouns are derived from verbs and retain the initial weak syllable. (For more details, see B2.)

Vocabulary notes
barrister = a lawyer who can appear in a higher court;
boozer = a person who likes alcoholic drinks (i.e. *booze*) far too much;
hack = a derogatory term for a journalist;
proctor = an official at the universities of Oxford and Cambridge;
solicitor = a lawyer who advises clients, prepares legal documents etc.

Tina's a **tea**cher, Pris**cil**la's a **prea**cher,
Donald's a **doc**tor and **Ted** drives a **truck**.
Fred's a pho**tog**rapher, **Joe**'s a ge**og**rapher,
Barry's a **bar**rister **down** on his **luck**.

Annie's an **an**archist, **Mon**ty's a **mon**archist,
Prue is a **proc**tor and **Fred** owns a **farm**.
Cy's a psy**chol**ogist, **Bill**'s a bi**ol**ogist,
Charley's a **char**mer who's **run** out of **charm**.

Col's a **col**lector and **Di**'s a di**rec**tor,
Astrid's an **as**tronaut, **Bas** runs a **bank**.
Con's a con**fes**sor and **Prue**'s a pro**fes**sor,
Cher owned a **ship** until (**sad**ly) it **sank**.

Mag's a ma**gi**cian and **Phil**'s a phy**si**cian,
Cosmo's a **cos**monaut **cir**cling the **moon**.
Ruby's a **re**alist, **Ike**'s an i**de**alist,
Cindy's a **sing**er who **can't** hold a **tune**.

Ruth is a **wri**ter and **Fred**dy's a **fight**er,
Phil's a phi**lanth**ropist **hand**ing out **cash**.
Sid's a psy**chot**ic and **Norm's** a neu**rot**ic,
Danny's a **dri**ver who's **scared** he might **crash**.

Walter's a **wai**ter and **Tom's** a trans**lat**or,
Aaron's an **air**man who **flies** through the **sky**.
Tammy's a **tai**lor and **Will**ie's a **whal**er,
Charlie's a **chair**man who **can't** tell a **lie**.

Benny's a **boo**zer and **Lenn**y's a **lo**ser,
Sol's a so**lic**itor, **Chlo**e's a **clown**.
Eddie's an **ed**itor, **Chriss**ie's a **cre**ditor,
Reg is a **wres**tler whose **job** gets him **down**.

Milly's a **mill**er and **Dave's** a dis**till**er,
Kate's a co**me**dian, **crack**ing a **joke**.
Dee is a **deal**er and **Harr**y's a **heal**er,
Dave is a **di**ver who **can't** swim a **stroke**.

Ben's a bal**loo**nist and **Bet's** a bas**soo**nist,
Freda's a **fem**inist, **Harr**y's a **hack**.
Zac's a zo**ol**ogist, **Tom's** a tech**no**logist,
Brenda's a **bro**ker who's **just** got the **sack**.

Sal's a se**lec**tor and **Den's** a de**fec**tor,
Mike is a **mi**ner all **co**vered in **grime**.
Rita's a **roy**alist, **Li**ta's a **loy**alist,
Paula's a **po**et whose **po**ems don't **rhyme**.

B1 ■ ○ nouns and adjectives

This stress pattern, which we may call **front (or early) stress**, is by far the most common both for nouns and for adjectives. And note how frequently nouns and adjectives of this type end with one of the weak syllables which we have already met in the case of ■ ○ verbs. E.g. luggage / manage / spillage / footage / mother / bother / father / cosy / hurry / fruity / window / callow / hollow / nimble / handle / partial / picture / treasure / seizure.

Notable among nouns of this type are those 'agentive' nouns derived from mono-syllabic verbs: diver / waiter / farmer / liar / player / teacher / actor etc.

Note: this includes that set of nouns (import / record / subject / refund / transfer / reject etc.) where the verbs with the same spelling have **late stress** e.g. to import / to record / to subject / to refund / to transfer / to reject

B2 nouns and adjectives derived from ○ ■ and ○ ■ ○ verbs

Most nouns and adjectives derived from ○ ■ and ○ ■ ○ verbs by the addition of suffixes, keep the same main stress as the verbs. There may, however, be a change of vowel sound and, occasionally, of consonant, e.g. to suffice / sufficiency; persuade / persuasion. (If the stress **does** change, then this is usually due to the presence of a suffix which imposes its own stress pattern, as we shall see later in this section.)

abandonment / accomplishment / accountable / amusing / behaviour / collection / comparison / defective / development / encirclement / enquiry / equipment / excitable / infectious / perversity / presumable / production / rehearsal / resemblance / sufficiency / transferral

This type again includes a large number of agentive nouns such as:

accountant / announcer / believer / dissembler / enquirer / offender / inquirer / inhabitant / producer / professor / protector / surveyor / transgressor

B3 Nouns and adjectives derived from ■ ○ verbs

Nouns and adjectives derived from ■ ○ verbs also tend to keep the stress pattern of the original verbs, e.g.

settlement / reckoning / censorship / management / manageable / banishment / nourishment / fellowship

Agentive nouns include:

caterer / creditor / editor / follower / idler / softener / manager / treasurer / wanderer

Note: the suffix <-ment> (found in catchment / bereavement / abandonment / management etc.), used to derive nouns from verbs, is stress neutral and pronounced with schwa. The sequence <-ment> is not always a suffix, however.

a) Some <-ment> nouns (including sentiment / detriment / element / instrument) do not derive from verbs.

b) Nor do a number of <-ment> words which can function as noun or verb, e.g.

    implement / compliment / complement / supplement / ornament

    As nouns the <-ment> ending has schwa, but as verbs it becomes /ment/.

Note however that native speakers do not always make this latter distinction.

B4 Stress-imposing suffixes

There are a number of suffixes which determine the stress pattern of nouns.

a) <-ion -ian > = /ən/ or /n/

In nouns ending with <ion> or <ian> the main stress falls on the syllable before the end, no matter how many syllables. Where these suffixes are found in words of four or more syllables, then there is a clear secondary stress:

nation / fusion / option / traction / fission / Asian / confusion / adoption / damnation / musician / technician / ˌcondemˈnation / ˌdisiˈllusion / ˌobsteˈtrician / ˌreabˈsorbtion / ˌcontraˈdiction / ˌompreˈhension / ˌintroˈduction / ˌappreˈhension / ˌindeˈcision / ˌproseˈcution / ˌsubstiˈtution / ˌaggraˈvation / reˌpudiˈation / conˌgratuˈlation / coˌordiˈnation / ˌmultipliˈcation / ˌrecommenˈdation / ˌrealiˈsation / ˌqualifiˈcation / ˌsimplifiˈcation / ˌmagnifiˈcation

Note how the syllable given secondary stress is usually that carrying main stress in the base verb, for example:

<-ate>	conˈgratulate	conˌgratuˈlation
<-ify>	ˈmagnify	ˌmagnifiˈcation
<-iply>	ˈmultiply	ˌmultipliˈcation
<-ise>	ˈrealise	ˌrealiˈsation

b) <-y> (●) (○) (○) ■ ○ ○

There are a large number of suffixes ending with <y>, corresponding to very weak /ɪ/. The preceding syllable also contains a very weak syllable, so the main stress comes two from the end, however long the word. These are similar in stress patterning to <-ly> adverbs, a selection of which are included for comparison.

A very high proportion of these nouns are formal and/or scientific or technical, containing such suffixes as: <-ory>, <-opy>, <-ocy>, <-acy>, <-apy>, <-ary>, <-athy>, <-omy>, <-ogy>, <-ophy>, <-aphy>, <-atry> and < -ity >.

■ ○ ○

therapy / ivory / history / oratory / secretary / canopy/ mystery / surgery / voluntary / apathy / sympathy / piety / lavatory / oracy
(gracefully / feelingly / hurriedly / seemingly / mercifully)

○ ■ ○ ○

identity / society / psychiatry / security / polygamy / psychology / gastronomy / philanthropy / biography / perversity / modernity / obituary / impiety / laboratory / authority / infirmity/ ethnicity
(amazingly / politically/ ungracefully / believably)

Note: this is the same stress pattern found in a number of 4-syllable words ending in <-e>, also corresponding to short /ɪ/. They include: apostrophe, epitome, catastrophe and hyperbole.

● ○ ■ ○ ○

,inca'pacity / ,capa'bility / ,regu'latory / ,elec'tricity / ,hagi'ography / ,cardi'ology / ,gene'alogy / ,multi'plicity / ,physi'ology /
(,under'standably / ,unbe'lievably / ,incon'ceivably)

● ○ ○ ■ ○ ○

,autobi'ography / ,parapsy'chology

Note that some words ending in <-y> (including *lavatory*, *literacy* and *secretary*) may have four syllables when spoken slowly. But in fast speech what is called **compression** may take place. This means that the schwa syllable may be elided, reducing the word to three syllables, possibly to fit other words with this pattern. In fact the middle schwa syllable in three syllable words, including *history* and *mystery* may similarly disappear. For example:

Item	Slow	Fast
lavatory	ˈlævətərɪ	ˈlævətrɪ
literacy	ˈlɪtərəsɪ	ˈlɪtrəsɪ
secretary	ˈsekrətərɪ	ˈsekrətrɪ
history	ˈhɪstərɪ	ˈhɪstrɪ
mystery	ˈmɪstərɪ	ˈmɪstrɪ

A moral tale

Here is a poem for you to practice your <-y> words. Don't worry about the meaning to start with. Just listen to it several times , then read it along with the tape, keeping to the same rhythm. When you are familiar with the sounds, check the meaning of the words in a dictionary. You will discover that it is a short story in the form of a poem: the story of a person born into a world of privilege for whom everything goes horribly wrong. All the words should be in the dictionary, except for *bitchery* which means 'spreading nasty stories about a person'.

ability
    heredity
        conformity
            maturity

      society
        authority
            monogamy
                security

        diversity
          duplicity
            adultery
               and bitchery

          publicity
            adversity
              infirmity
                obituary

c) <-ographer>, <-onomer>, <-onomist> <-iatrist>

The very productive b) group (see page 43) includes those learned suffixes: <-ology>, <-onomy> <-ography> <-iatry>. These have corresponding agentive nouns with the same stress pattern, e.g.

> phot**O**grapher / bi**O**grapher / a**stro**nomer / bi**ol**ogist / psy**chi**atrist / e**con**omist / a**gron**omist / ˌhagi'**O**grapher / ˌparapsy'**cho**logist etc.

Note that the syllable following the main stress always contains schwa; thus phot**O**grapher = fə'tɒgrəfə; a**gron**omist = ə'grɒnəmist

d) <-ese> /iːz/

The <-ese> suffix is found in a number of nationality words (including Chi**nese** / Japa**nese** / Vietna**mese**) as well as a few other words such as journa**lese**.

e) <-esque> /esk/ and <-ette> /et/

These suffixes are fairly rare. The first is used to derive adjectives from a number of proper names, to give the meaning 'similar to, in the style of' e.g. *Kafkaesque* / *Goyaesque* / *Chaplinesque*. (It is also found in a few other adjectives and nouns, such as *picturesque* and *humoresque*.) The second is found as a diminutive suffix in such words as *cigarette*, *kitchenette*, *lecturette* and *laundrette*.

> Note that <-ese> , <-esque> and <-ette> impose a secondary stress two syllables before the main stress: e.g. ˌjapa'**nese** / ˌpictu'**resque** / ˌciga'**rette**.

f) <-ic >, <-ics>, <-ical>, <-icist >

These related suffixes, all containing <ic>, affect the stress pattern of a large number of nouns and adjectives. The rule is that main stress falls on the syllable immediately before. For example:

> ■ ○ (○)
>
> **pu**blic(ist) / **cy**nic(al) / **to**pic(al) / **lo**gic(al) / **op**tics / **op**tic(al) / **phy**sic(al) / **phy**sics / **phy**sicist / **cau**stic / **tra**gic / **cri**tic(al) / **cla**ssic(al) / **eth**nic

> ○ ■ ○ (○)
>
> ce**ram**ic(s) / ce**ram**icist / hy**drau**lic(s) / e**lec**tric(al) / cos**me**tic(s) / dy**na**mic / an**ge**lic / dy**nas**tic / mes**me**ric / his**to**ric(al) / aes**the**tic / ar**tis**tic / pa**the**tic / po**li**tical / i**llo**gical
>
> Exceptions **po**litic(s) / **lu**natic / **A**rabic

● ○ ■ ○ (○)

,mathe'matics / ,peri'odic(al) / ,geri'atric(s) / ,eco'nomic(s) /
,eco'nomic(al) / ,hydro'ponic(s) / ,meta'physics / ,meta'physical /
,anaes'thetic / ,ano'rexic / ,oce'anic / ,aca'demic / ,narci'ssistic /
,mathe'matical / ,astro'nomical / ,cate'goric(al)

● ● ○ ○ ■ ○

,geria'trician / ,paedia'trician

B5 <-ist>

This is used to derive adjectives from:

1 **nouns:** machinist / balloonist / bassoonist etc. or

2 **adjectives:** realist / loyalist / royalist / idealist etc.

Note: Careful with the suffix <-al> !

When used to derive nouns from verbs it is stress neutral (e.g. refuse / refusal; approve / approval). But when used to derive adjectives from nouns it imposes stress, usually on the preceding syllable. (e.g. sentiment / sentimental; detriment / detrimental; element / elemental; instrument / instrumental; ornament / ornamental; universe / universal.)

Careful, too with <-able>, which is used to derive adjectives from certain verbs. It is usually stress-neutral (e.g. allow / allowable; desire /desirable; bribe / bribable; forget / forgettable / unforgettable etc). But a number of common adjectives break this rule: admirable and preferable, notably. And usage varies in the case of a number of words, including *comparable*, *applicable* and *transferable*.

C Stress in compounds and phrases

Compounds are composed of more than one word or element, whether written as one word or not. And it is the main syllable in the first element of compounds which has primary stress.

C1 *Most compound **nouns** are made up of two elements, usually **noun + noun**. For example:*

postman / policeman / teapot / classroom / bus stop / egghead / nosejob / schoolgirl / landlady / bookshop / brainstorm / 'evening ,dress / means test / hitchhiker / bloodsucker / mathe'matics ,teacher / 'tennis ,player / 'English ,teacher (= teacher of English) / 'visitors ,book / 'children's ,home / 'parents ,evening / etc.

But other combinations of elements are possible.

C2 adjective + noun *(very common)*

redhead / greenback / shortbread / longboat / greenhouse / bighead / hardware / bluebottle / shorthand / smalltalk / broadside / hotspot / the 'White ,House / two-step / four-ply / six-pack / hundredweight / etc.

C3 gerund + noun *(very common)*

dining-room / swimming pool / baking powder / moving van / breathing space / running track / ironing board / skipping rope / winning post / etc.

C4 verb + particle *(increasingly common)*

take off / shutdown / standby / sit-in / putdown / follow-up / walkout / flyover / drive-in / talkback / turn up / wind-up / flyby / breakthrough / sit up / stop over / hand over / etc.

C5 verb + noun *(not very common)*

cut-throat / driveway / runway / makeweight / drophead / swimwear /etc.

C6 particle + verb *(not very common)*

offcut / input / offspring / overpass / underwear / bypass / throughput / etc.

C7 two elements from Latin or Greek *(very common, especially in formal and/or scientific language)*

autocrat / acrobat / photograph / telephone / synonym / symphony / lithograph / microphone / biopsy / homophone / technocrat / gramophone / isobar / epigram / acronym / paragraph / thermostat / etc.

The meaning of most **noun + noun compounds** is usually quite clear; both constituents are ordinary English words and the compound is the sum of both words. Thus a *bookshop* is 'a shop where you buy books', a *bus-stop* is 'a place where buses stop'.

The meaning of **element + element compounds** is usually less obvious. But words such as *autograph*, *biopsy* and *telephone* contain highly meaningful elements: *auto* = 'self'; *graph* = 'writing '; *bio* = 'life'; *tele* = 'far', and *phone* = 'sound'.

The meanings of elements such as these are well worth knowing. They are only occasionally found as independent words. In combination, however, they produce several thousand 3-syllable words, all with front stress and a very weak second syllable. (Of course, they are found in longer words, too; an *autobiography* – 'self' + 'life' + 'writing' – is 'an account of a person's life written by that person her- or himself'.) Since these elements are often neglected, I have written a poem to help you learn a number of them.

Task seventeen

A poem is often divided into separate **stanzas** (also called, **verses**). The following poem is written in what is known as **rhyming couplets**. (A **couplet** is a two-line stanza, so **rhyming couplets** are couplets where the rhyme scheme is AA BB CC etc.) Here are the first two couplets of the poem:

An **ac**robat is agile and can somersault and leap;
An **oc**topus is something you might see beneath the deep.

A **ther**mostat is useful to control the rate of heat;
A **met**ronome is what you need to help you keep the beat

As you can see, each line contains the definition of a 3-syllable classical compound. (With front stress, of course.) Each compound is in its correct position in the poem below, but the definitions have been jumbled up. Your task is to:

● listen to the poem once or twice to get the rhythm;

● use a good dictionary to check the meaning of each compound;

● find the continuation which matches the meaning of the compound;

● re-create the poem.

Notes on the main elements found in the poem.

\<anthrop\>	= 'human'	anthropoid, philanthropist, etc.
\<aqua\>	= 'water'	aquatic, aquaduct, etc.
\<astr\>	= 'star'	astroid, astro–physics, astronaut, etc.
\<auto\>	= 'self'	automatic, automobile, etc.
\<chrom\>	= 'colour'	monochromatic, polychromatic, etc.
\<cide\>	= 'kill'	homicide, regicide, germicide, etc.
\<duc\>	= 'lead, take'	duct, deduct, conduct, deduce, etc.
\<cosm\>	= 'world'	cosmic, microcosm, etc.
\<glot\>	= 'language'	glottis, polyglot, monoglot, etc.
\<gogue\>	= 'leader'	pedagogue, demagogue, etc.
\<graph\>	= 'writing'	telegraph, graphic, paragraph, etc.
\<homo\>	= 'same'	homophone, homograph, homosexual, etc.
\<hydro\>	= 'water'	hydro–electric, dehydrate, hydrogen, etc.
\<hypno\>	= 'sleep'	hypnosis, hypnotherapy, etc.
\<micro\>	= 'small'	microphone, microscopic, microcosm, etc.
\<mono\>	= 'one'	monocle, monotonous, monocellular, etc.
\<morph\>	= 'shape'	amorphous, morphology, anthropomorphic, etc.
\<naut\>	= 'sail, travel'	nautical, cosmonaut, astronaut, etc.
\<oid\>	= 'shaped like'	anthropoid, spheroid, ovoid, humanoid, etc.
\<ped\>	= 'child'	pedagogue, paediatrics, pederast, etc.
		(NB \<ped\> also = 'foot', as in pedal, pedestrian)
\<peri\>	= 'around'	perimeter, periscope, perigastric, etc.
\<phone\>	= 'sound'	telephone, phonetics, microphone, etc.
\<photo\>	= 'light'	photograph, photo–sensitive, etc.
\<poly\>	= 'many'	polymorph, polyglot, polytheism, etc.
\<reg\>	= 'king'	regicide, regal, reign, etc.
\<scope\>	= 'vision'	telescope, microscope, etc.
\<tele\>	= 'far'	telescope, telephone, telegram, etc.
\<via\>	= 'road'	viaduct, viable, deviate, etc.

An acrobat is agile

An **ac**robat is agile and can somersault and leap;
An **oc**topus is something you might see beneath the deep.

A **ther**mostat is useful to control the rate of heat;
A **met**ronome is what you need to help you keep the beat

1 A **per**iscope is   **a)** something that can take on many shapes
2 A **chro**mosome is   **b)** pick up every single word you say

3 A **ho**mophone's   **c)** a type of boat that skims across the sea
4 A **te**legram is   **d)** useful if you want to see a wreck

5 A **po**lymorph is   **e)** for people who like dancing every day
6 The **an**thropoids are   **f)** occasionally worn by certain men

7 A **te**lephone's   **g)** teach your little children, for a fee
8 A **mi**crophone can   **h)** found in living cells, just like a gene

9 A **hy**drofoil's   **i)** what will bring you water from afar
10 A **pe**dagogue will   **j)** visit Venus, Jupiter or Mars

11 A **cos**monaut might   **k)** never even dream of such a thing
12 An **as**tronaut could   **l)** something you can use to trap a liar

13 A **ger**micide is   **m)** someone who has killed a queen or king
14 A **disco**theque's   **n)** known to certain people as a 'snap'

15 A **pho**tograph is   **o)** written with a pencil or a pen
16 A **hyp**notist is   **p)** useful if you're in a submarine

17 A **po**lyglot might   **q)** something that you might send to your
                      mother

18 A **ba**thysphere is   **r)** go much farther, even to the stars

19 The **di**nosaurs   **s)** shaped like us: the monkeys and the apes
20 while **hy**drogen   **t)** understand both Japanese and Czech
    and **ox**ygen

21 An **aqu**aduct is   **u)** by contrast, is more useful for your car
22 A **via**duct,   **v)** someone who could help you take a nap

23 An **au**tograph is   **w)** things you shouldn't throw into a fire
24 A **mo**nocle's   **x)** combine as H_2O

25 A **po**lygraph is   **y)** a word that sounds exactly like another
26 and **ae**rosols are   **z)** for talking to a person far away

27 A **reg**icide is   **aa)** what can help to keep disease at bay
28 A **mon**archist would   **bb)** all died out several million years ago

And if this kind of **lex**icon is hard to comprehend,
then you had better try to get a teacher as a friend.

Note: those compound nouns which can also be used as verbs retain front stress (to 'brainstorm, to 'whitewash, to 'blackball, to 'means test, to 'photograph, to 'telephone, to 'bypass, to 'input etc.).

But compare with equivalent phrasal verbs which have late stress, e.g. to ,take 'off, ,walk 'out etc.

Note that a compound can itself be the first element in a longer compound, thus: 'ballroom ,dancer / 'telephone ,operator / 'swimming-pool a,ttendant / 'football ,match / 'underwear ,salesman / 'shutdown pro,cedure / 'ironing board ,cover / 'software de,velopment / 'teapot ,cover etc.

C8 Stress in noun phrases

Two-word noun phrases tend to have **late stress** . We can say that, within the phrase, the first element has secondary stress while the second has primary stress.

Many two-word phrases consist of the same elements found in compounds: noun + noun; adjective + noun; gerund + noun. And sometimes the actual words used are the same in both compound and phrase. So it is worth looking at the underlying differences in meaning.

Task eighteen

Look at the following pairs of sentences. In each pair, the first sentence contains a phrase, and the second a compound. See if you can work out the differences in meaning.

1 She was wearing a ,cotton 'dress.
   They work in a 'cotton ,factory.

2 You should be wearing ,rubber 'gloves.
   I've just bought a 'rubber ,plant.

3 Would you like a ,meat 'pie?
   He works as a 'meat ,packer.

4 I've invited two friends, an ,English 'teacher (and a French scientist).
   She works as an 'English ,teacher.

5 We saw a beautiful ,black 'bird.
   We saw a beautiful 'blackbird.

6 Can you see that ,white 'house over there?
   The US President lives in the 'White ,House.

7 It's dangerous to jump on to a ,moving 'train.
   We have so much furniture we'll need a 'moving ,van.

8 I put all my money on the ,winning 'horse!
   The horses are very close to the 'winning ,post.

So it seems that **phrases** tend to mean either:

1 X is made of Y   (*a meat pie, cotton dress, rubber gloves*, etc.) or
2 X is Y   (*an English teacher, a winning horse, a white house*, etc.)

And **compounds**, by contrast, tend to mean either:

1 X is a special type of Y (*a blackbird, the White House*, etc.)
2 X is for Y   (*a cotton factory, dining-room, moving-van*, etc.)
3 an X of Y   (*a meat packer, an English teacher*)

> **Note:** These are tendencies which cover the great majority of cases. But be careful of the words *cake*, *juice* and *water*. They do not obey the X is made of Y rule. For example:
>
> phrases: a ˌcheese ˈsandwich / an ˌapple ˈpie / a ˌbarley ˈloaf
>
> compounds: a ˈcheesecake / an ˈorange ˌjuice / some ˈbarley ˌwater
>
> And the sequences ˌwinter ˈdress / ˌsummer ˈsuit / ˌspring ˈhat etc. are phrases, although they could be explained as meaning 'a dress for the winter', 'a suit for the summer' etc.

> **Note** also that late stress is found in such phrases as:
>
> a ˌcup of ˈtea / a ˌpint of ˈmilk / a ˌpound of ˈbutter /
>
> a ˌbottle of ˈbeer / ˌrock and ˈroll / ˌfish and ˈchips / ˌham and ˈeggs /
>
> ˌboys and ˈgirls etc.

> **Note**, finally, that sequences may consist of a **combination** of **phrase** and **compound**. Thus the phrase ˌhot ˈwater can be the first part of the compound ˌhot ˈwater ˌbottle. By contrast, the compound ˈelderflower can be the first part of the phrase ˌelderflower chamˈpagne.

A cautionary tale

Task nineteen

Here is a poem containing a number of noun compounds and phrases.

● Read it first and see if you can identify which are the compounds and which are the phrases among the things which Alexandra buys.

● Then listen to it and see if your ears confirm what your eyes see.

Vocabulary notes

Clothes terms

The following three words are all from French: *brassiere* (worn to support the breasts); *lingerie* (= 'women's underwear'); a *negligee* (a light garment, usually worn over a night-dress). *Hose* is a technical term for socks, tights and stockings.

acquire is a formal word meaning 'to get, obtain, receive'; *attire* is a very formal word meaning 'clothes'; *distraught* (rhymes with thought/taught/caught) = 'worried, nervous'; *expire* is a formal word meaning 'to die' (a visa or licence can expire.); *flashy* means 'too bright, in bad taste'; to *hoard* = 'to hide something away' (a *hoard* is what is hidden); *hues* = 'colours'; something *illicit* is what you do not want people to know about; to *let* a person *down* = 'to disappoint them'; a *shopping spree* is when you spend a lot of money buying things; *sombre* is the opposite of 'bright'; *spouse* is a formal word meaning 'husband or wife'; *stifled* means 'cut off', as if a hand is put over your mouth.

One morning Alexandra Brown
got on the bus and went to town.
Convinced she looked a total mess
she thought she'd buy a cheapish dress.
But she had recently acquired
a credit card, and thus inspired
set off upon a shopping spree
from nine o'clock till half past three.

She started in a modest way;
a cotton skirt, in darkish grey.
But what it needed, so she felt,
would be a simple leather belt.
But when the belt was fastened tight
she thought it called for something bright;
a brooch, a ring, some earrings too,
two silken blouses, pink and blue.

And then, her shoes, a sombre green,
were hardly worthy to be seen;
she really needed one more pair
(she scarcely had a thing to wear).
But hesitating which to buy
she finally decided, 'I
will take the black, the blue, the brown,
(they're always nice around the town)
and then those white ones, and the peach
(just right for summer on the beach).

And since I'd like to take up sport
well then, perhaps I think I ought
to buy myself some tennis shoes
and I suppose I'd better choose
some riding breeches and a skirt
with just a simple linen shirt.'

And so she went from store to store,
just thinking 'maybe one thing more'.
From Selfridges to C & A
(well, after all, no need to pay)
Armani, Harrods, BHS
'Well that's the lot', she thought, 'unless
I bought myself an evening gown.
I really can't let Crispin down.
A handbag, too', then for a laugh
she chose a rather flashy scarf.

'And that is that,' at last she thought,
now feeling just a touch distraught.
'I'd better get home for my tea.
I wonder what the bill will be.'

The following month the bill appeared;
it was far worse than she had feared.
Ten thousand pounds and twenty p.
'Oh dear, ' she murmured, 'Goodness me!'
'Now what will Crispin think? Oh my!
He'll want to know the reason why.'
(She'd hidden all her things away,
afraid of what her spouse would say.)

Then suddenly she had a thought;
surely the things that she had bought
could all be taken back and then
things would be normal once again!

She rushed up to the second floor
and placed her hand upon the door
of that large wardrobe where she'd stored
the whole of her illicit hoard.
She grabbed the handle, gave a twist
with all the power of her wrist.

The door flew wide, and suddenly
out came a flood of lingerie,
of coats and hats and tights and shoes,
and brassieres of different hues,
of summer blouses, winter hose,
an avalanche of varied clothes,
of cashmere sweaters, fine and rare,
of overcoats and underwear.
She tried to scream, she tried to shout,
she tried to wave her arms about,
but under piles of mixed attire
she started slowly to expire.
Her final little cry of 'hey!'
was stifled by a negligee.

So when you're going out to shop
and want to ask for credit, stop!
Just listen carefully to my tip
and think before you sign the slip.

C9 Stress in adjectival compounds and phrases

Adjectives, like nouns can be found both in early-stressed compounds and in late-stressed phrases. Here are some examples of both.

C10 Adjectival compounds

a) noun + adjective

The soldiers were so 'bloodthirsty they killed everyone in the village.

They are so 'houseproud they spend all their time cleaning and polishing.

He's broken his leg again. He's really 'accident-prone.

b) noun + gerund

The horror film was very 'blood-curdling.

That fruit is very 'thirst-quenching.

The Grand Canyon is really 'awe-inspiring.

c) noun + past participle

> After months at sea she was completely 'sun-tanned.
>
> Stand up for yourself. You've been 'down-trodden all your life.
>
> Shy? I was absolutely 'tongue-tied.
>
> I'm afraid our cats aren't 'toilet-trained.

C11 Adjectival phrases

a) adjective + past participle

> They're so ˌabsent 'minded they even forget their children's names!
>
> They are so ˌlow-'paid they never go away on holiday.
>
> I like my eggs ˌhard-'boiled, five minutes at least.
>
> I wouldn't trust her. She's completely ˌtwo-'faced.

b) adjective + gerund

> You can relax with them. They're really ˌeasy-'going.
>
> He's ˌgood-'looking with excellent dress-sense.

c) adjective + noun

> Her novels are really ˌfirst-'class, but her plays are pretty ˌsecond-'rate.
>
> The job is really ˌhigh-'risk.

d) adjective + adjective

> Careful! That iron is ˌred-'hot!
>
> He was lying in the road ˌdead 'drunk.

e) adjective/past participle + particle

> I can't lend you a penny, I'm afraid. I'm rather ˌhard-'up at the moment.
>
> I've had enough. I'm really ˌfed-'up; completely ˌbrowned-'off!
>
> I'm not just ˌtired-'out; I'm ˌall-'in.

f) adverb + adjective/past participle

> She's ,**fantastically** '**cl**ever and really ,**well-**'**known**.
>
> His questions are always ,**carefully** '**cho**sen.

g) particle + past participle

> I like my meat ,**under** '**done** but that was really ,**over-**'**cooked**.

h) three-word phrases

> Don't let this go any further. It's strictly ,**off-the-**'**re**cord.
>
> He has no self-control. His performance was really ,**over-the-**'**top**.
>
> Their clothes are always ,**up to** '**date**.
>
> The novel is pretty ,**down to** '**earth**.
>
> You can come when you like. The rules aren't ,**hard and** '**fast**.
>
> The acting is inconsistent; very ,**hit and** '**miss**.

i) noun + adjective

> Their clothes were ,**brand-**'**new**.
>
> Eat up or your food will be ,**stone-**'**cold**.
>
> All our eggs are ,**farm-**'**fresh**.

j) noun + past participle

> All our beer is ,**home-**'**brewed** and our pullovers are ,**hand-**'**knit**ted.
>
> The knives and forks are ,**silver-**'**plat**ed.
>
> She won't change her mind. She's really ,**iron** '**willed**.

As you can see, the choice between compound and phrase is clear except where you have **noun + adjective/past participle**. In such cases you just have to learn the stress pattern when learning the item, I'm afraid.

> **Note** that **adverbial phrases** tend to have late stress, e.g.
>
> He tripped and fell ,**head-over** '**heels**.   We talked ,**round the** '**clock**.
>
> We rowed ,**down** '**stream**.   Let's meet ,**half-**'**way**.
>
> She answered us ,**absent-**'**min**dedly.

D Stress patterns in words and phrases

Here are various stress patterns. Listen to the recording, then listen and repeat. Note that most patterns can be represented either by a single word or by a longer sequence: a phrase (or even a sentence).

1 ■	watched	James
2 ■○	wanted	drop it
3 ○■	forgive	a bird
4 ●■	come in	ten men
5 ■○○	Saturday	lots of them
6 ○■○	develop	below them
7 ○○■	for an hour	to the bank
8 ●○■	introduce	rock and roll
9 ●○■○	Alexander	look around you
10 ●○○■	Lewisham Road	come to the door
11 ○■○○	photographer	a lot of them
12 ●○○■○	magnification	Westminster Abbey
13 ●○■○○	incapacity	in the library
14 ●○○■○○	parapsychology	into the library

Task twenty

Now look at the following words, names and phrases; read them aloud; and number them according to their stress pattern.

somebody	police	photographic
go to the bank	stopped	Kensington High Street
Vaughan	Hungary	defend
leather	Speaker's Corner	biology
Charing Cross	a big one	best results
institution	try a banana	Elizabeth
tomato	buy a new one	for a while
Madonna	biographical	Leicester
conservative	Buckingham Palace	Royal Exchange

inner circle	offer him money	buy now
knives	all of the elephants	Michael
Peru	geriatrician	after it
through	half a sandwich	to the school
Iran	a pound of it	Madame Tussauds
a few	outer space	autobiography
Manchester	next year	Trafalgar
Macbeth	hungry	dead drunk
follow	Peter Davidson	half a pound
embargo	sympathy	buy us some food
tired out	give me a drink	sending a telegram
maternity	the last of them	Nelson's Column
red hot	come to the disco	disability
as a rule	policeman	

E Stress shift

So far we have assumed that each word could only be stressed in one way. But there are circumstances in which the rules of stress are broken and stress can shift from its normal place.

E1 Contrastive stress shift

Firstly, any stress pattern can change if we want to show a particular contrast. Thus the word *policeman* is normally pronounced /pəˈliːsmən/, with main stress on the first element, as is usual in compounds. But see what happens in the following exchange.

1 So a po**lic**eman came to see you, did he? (= /pəˈliːsmən/)
   No, not a police**man**; it was a police**wo**man, (= /pəˌliːsˈmæn/)

The contrast between *man* and *woman* over-rides the normal rule. Here are some more examples of contrastive stress shift.

2 So you've bought a new **te**lephone. /ˈtələfəʊn/
   No, not a tele**phone**, a tele**scope**. /ˌteləˈfəʊn/

3 I gather that John's a **phy**sics teacher. /ə ˈfɪzɪks ˌtiːtʃə/
   No, he's a physics **stud**ent, not a physics **teach**er. /əˌfɪzɪks ˈtiːtʃə/

4 You're a com**pu**ter operator, I understand.
No, not a computer **op**erator, a computer **pro**grammer.

5 Would you like a cheese **sand**wich?
I'd rather have a to**ma**to sandwich.

6 Would you like to sit out**side**?
Is it possible to sit **in**side, instead?

7 Did you buy that cotton **shirt** you were looking at?
No, I changed my mind and bought a **silk** shirt.

8 Do you fancy fish and **chips**?
I'd rather have **chick**en and chips, I think.

9 As a writer, I'd rate him first-**class**. What do you think?
Closer to **third**-class, in my opinion.

Let's see what has happened to the **stress patterns** in the above examples.

a) Compounds can lose their front stress, which can give them the stress pattern associated with phrases.

'telephone   tele'phone (2)

'physics ,teacher   ,physics 'teacher (3)

b) Or the opposite can happen, with phrases having the pattern associated with compounds.

to,mato 'sandwich   to'mato ,sandwich (5)

,chicken and 'chips   'chicken and ,chips

But careful. Spoken language is more than just stress, as has already been said. So we have to do more than just shift the stress. Here are some of those sequences again. Listen once more, this time paying particular attention to the **intonation** in the second sentence of each example.

1 So a po**li**ceman came to see you, did he?

No, not a police**man**; it was a police**wo**man.

2 So you've bought a new **te**lephone.

No, not a tele**phone**, a tele**scope**.

3 I gather that John's a **phy**sics teacher.

No, he's a physics **stud**ent, not a physics **teach**er.

4 You're a com**pu**ter operator, I understand.

No, a computer **pro**grammer, not a computer **op**erator.

The first speaker in each case not only uses the regular stress pattern for *policeman*, *telephone*, *physics teacher* and *computer operator*; s/he also uses a **falling tone**. This is the normal tone in such cases; **new** information is being introduced into the conversation. But when the sequences are repeated by the second speaker we have to note, not only the shift of stress, but also the use of **a fall-rise tone**. This is because the items are now part of **old, shared** information. When the second speaker supplies **new** information (*policewoman*, *telescope*, *student*, *programmer*) s/he uses, as we might expect, the **falling** tone again.

So, from now on, do not pay so much attention to stress that you neglect intonation. In particular, when you listen to (and imitate) the poems in Part 4 make sure you concentrate not only on getting the beat, but on making sure that you have a feel for the rhythm of English; the music of English is there, too.

E2 Forward stress shift

Secondly, the stress can change according to what is happening in the rest of the sentence. Listen to the following sequences.

You need a **first**-class ticket to travel first-**class**.
Princess Elizabeth's a royal prin**cess**.
I live in Picca**dil**ly, near **Pi**ccadilly Circus.
My friend's Chin**ese**, she's a **Chi**nese cook.
Her **six**teenth birthday is on the six**teenth**.
You're always inter**fer**ing, you **in**terfering fool!
I work out**doors**, I've got an **out**door job.
He's really shar**p-eyed**; he's a **sharp**-eyed guy.
She works part-**time**, she's got a **part**-time position.
I've got a **rent**-free house, I live rent-**free**.
He's a **small**-time gambler, really small **time**.
It's nine o'**clock**, let's listen to the **nine** o'clock news.
We must be demo**crat**ic, take a **de**mocratic vote!
I agree abso**lute**ly, I'm **ab**solutely sure.
The book's una**bridged**, it's the **un**abridged version.

Have you worked out what happens? Most phrases, as we have seen, have late stress, as do a large number of words when in their dictionary form or at the end of a sequence. But **the stress shifts forward** when the phrase or word acts as a modifier within another phrase.[1] If the explanation sounds complicated, just listen and compare the two types on the opposite page.

---

1 This usually happens within noun phrases, but it can happen within other types of phrase, as you can see from the example of *absolutely sure*.

word or phrase	longer phrase containing the original
ˌfirst-'class	a ˌfirst-class 'ticket
a ˌprin'cess	ˌPrincess E'lizabeth
ˌPicca'dilly	ˌPiccadilly 'Circus
ˌChi'nese	a ˌChinese 'cook
ˌsix'teenth	her ˌsixteenth 'birthday
ˌinter'fering	you ˌinterfering 'fool
ˌout'doors	an ˌoutdoor 'job
ˌshar'p-eyed	a ˌsharp-eyed 'guy
ˌpart-'time	a ˌpart-time po'sition.
ˌrent-'free	a ˌrent-free 'house
ˌsmall 'time	a ˌsmall-time 'gambler
ˌnine o'clock	the ˌnine o'clock 'news.
ˌdemo'cratic	a ˌdemocratic 'vote
ˌuna'bridged	the ˌunabridged 'version.
ˌabso'lutely	ˌabsolutely 'sure

The modifier in the right-hand column is marked as having secondary stress. That is to show what it does within the phrase; the primary stress comes in the main word of the phrase.

A long-haired drummer in a rock 'n' roll band.

Task twenty-one

● Listen to and then repeat the following 4-beat poem/chant.

● Note down every example of a phrase in which stress shift has taken place.

Vocabulary notes
There are several words associated with show business in general or rock/jazz music in particular. A *gig* is a concert or other event when you get paid to play; a *fan* is a person who likes your music; a *lick* is a musical phrase; you play the bass-drum by foot, using a *pedal*; to *hit it big* is to become popular and successful; the *stand* (or band-stand) is a raised platform where the band plays; to *get a hand* is to be clapped or applauded by the audience.

1 I worked last night, played a one-night stand.
  I'm a long-haired drummer in a rock 'n' roll band.

2 It was a four-hour show, a first-rate gig.
  Some day soon we should be hitting it big.

3 The crowd all cheered, we got a well-earned hand;
  especially the drummer in the rock 'n' roll band.

4 A red-headed woman wearing high-heeled shoes
  helped a bald-headed fellow dance away his blues.

5 An unnamed fan clambered on the stand
  to try to reach the drummer of the rock 'n' roll band.

6 We were stone-cold sober, didn't touch a drop,
  had no time for drinking, we were playing non-stop.

7 It was positively great, it was absolutely grand
  to be drumming as a member of a rock 'n' roll band.

8 We played instrumental numbers, all the rock 'n' roll licks
  I smashed my bass-drum pedal and a dozen pairs of sticks.

9 They wouldn't let us go, we played longer than we planned.
  You'd think they'd never danced to a rock 'n' roll band.

10 Five, four, three, two a one-night stand.
   I'm a long-haired drummer in a rock 'n' roll band.

In this final section of Part 2 we have been looking at the ways in which the rules of stress can change.

But other things can change, too, especially in fast, informal speech. And that is what we will be looking at in Part 3.

Part 3

PART 3

FAST, NATURAL SPEECH

Introduction

So far we have looked at the following areas: the importance of stress; vowel length; the way words link together; rules of stress, both in words and phrases; and the times when rules can be over-ridden.

All of the above are important, however slow or however fast the rate of speaking, however formal or informal the occasion. What we have been looking at, in fact, are the things that you **must** do when speaking English if you want to be understood easily.

In this part we will look at what happens when English is spoken at normal, fast speed. Not in very formal contexts, such as making speeches or giving lectures, but in the normal, everyday situations of life.

Of course you do not have to try to speak this fast. You can carry on speaking relatively slowly and – provided that you stress words and phrases accurately – people will understand your pronunciation.

But if you want to understand normal, fast English, then it is important for you to pay attention to what is covered here. And, of course, if you want to approach native-speaker speed, then you must practise what is covered here.

In other words: Parts 1 and 2 contain what you must learn if you want **us** to understand **you**. And this part contains what you must learn:

a) if **you** want to understand **us**, and

b) if you want to begin to really **sound** like us.

In a moment we will begin to look in detail at the different things that happen when we speak English fast. But there is one thing that they all have in common: they make it **easier** to speak fast.

When we speak we use a large number of different muscles, sometimes at the same time. And as we do with any type of repeated physical activity, we try to cut down on unnecessary movements; we take short cuts. The opening two tasks in this section are to see if you can hear some of the main differences between slow and fast speech. And one of the things that happens, when we start to speak faster, is that certain sounds **disappear**. So the first task in this section is to see if you can hear when this happens.

Task twenty-two

You will hear the same passage read twice. First slowly, then fast. Listen to both versions carefully then decide which sounds are heard in the slow version but are not heard in the fast version.

The first girl and the first boy
The second girl and the second boy
The third girl and the third boy
The next girl and the next boy
The last girl and the last boy

Task twenty-three

The second thing that happens when we begin to speak fast is that certain sounds **change**. Listen again to the two passages and decide which sounds are different in the fast version.

Tasks 22 and 23 showed the two main types of change that take place when we speak fast. And from now on we will call these changes by their usual names. (Don't be worried about technical terms; there aren't many of them, they save a lot of time, and you will get used to them very quickly.)

Type 1 Elision
Elision is when a sound simply disappears (= **is elided**).
There is a small set of sounds – always the same – which tend to be elided when we speak fast, but only in a specific set of circumstances.

Type 2 Assimilation
Assimilation is what happens when a sound changes (= **is assimilated**) because of another sound. There are two main forms of assimilation:

a) a sound changes to become more like the next sound; this is called **anticipatory assimilation**;

b) two sounds join together to become a third sound; this is called **coalescent assimilation** (= the two sounds merge, or **coalesce**, to become one).

In the rest of Part 3 we will be looking in detail at elision and assimilation. But first, here is a version of the 'First girl, first boy' sequence, extended into a chant. Listen to it several times, then chant along with it. You will find that you can only keep up (i.e. chant at the same speed) if you do what a native speaker does: hit the stress correctly, weaken vowels where necessary, link, elide and assimilate. Look out in particular for the weak forms of *that*, *a*, *of* and *was*, all containing schwa.

Don't worry if you don't get the point of the elision and assimilation immediately; we will look at both of them later in this section.

Vocabulary notes

Cooking or preparing food
You *fry* food (eggs, meat, bread etc.) in a *frying-pan* with fat or oil.
You *grill* food over or under direct heat. A barbecue is a type of *grill*.
You *slice* bread (cake, meat etc.) with a knife. You can buy *sliced* bread and can eat a *slice of cake*. You *toast* slices of bread under a grill or in an electric *toaster* until they are brown. (Toasted bread is called *toast*.)

Talking
To *boast* is to talk with pride about what you do or own, about your family etc.
To *mutter* is to talk quietly and indistinctly, so that people find it hard to understand.
To *trill* is to produce two different sounds very fast, rather like a bird.

The first girl said that she'd like a slice of bread.
The second girl muttered that she'd really like it buttered.
The third girl replied that she'd rather have it fried.
The next girl trilled that she much preferred it grilled.
The last girl was quiet ... but she was on a diet.

The first boy said that he'd like a slice of bread.
The second boy muttered that he'd really like it buttered.
The third boy replied that he'd rather have it fried.
The next boy trilled that he much preferred it grilled.
The last boy was quiet ... but he was on a diet.

A Elision

A1 Elision of /t/ and /d/

In Task 22 we saw that in fast speech the sounds /t/ and /d/ were elided in contexts such as: *firs(t) girl / firs(t) boy / secon(d) girl / secon(d) boy*

The context which is common to all four – and which makes elision likely – is that /d/ and /t/ were found:

a) at the end of a word, and

b) between two other consonants.

Task twenty-four

Read the following sequences. See if you can identify where /d/ and /t/ elision can take place when they are read fast.

1 The morning was perfect.

2 It was a perfect morning.

3 It was a perfectly marvellous morning.

4 What does she want?

5 She wants ten pounds of butter.

6 I find it interesting, but he finds it boring.

7 We need to have the facts as soon as possible.

8 I don't usually watch television, but I watched four different programmes last night.

9 Jane hates fast food, so she won't want any burgers.

10 We're having roast beef with baked potatoes and beans.

Some effects of /d/ and /t/ elision

1 You hear the final /d/ or /t/ in the root of some words, but not when a suffix is added. For example:

Without elision	With elision
It was perfect	It was perfec(t)ly marvellous
That's exact	That's exac(t)ly right
She's full of tact	She's very tac(t)ful
What does she want?	She wan(t)s some butter
One pound of butter	Ten poun(d)s of butter

2 Elision can also affect the <-ed> for simple past and past participle. This means that, at speed, there may be no difference between present and past simple. (The context is what makes the difference clear, of course.)

slow version	fast version
I watch television every day.	I watch television every day.
I watched television last night.	I watch(ed) television last night.
They crash the car regularly.	They crash the car regularly.
They crashed the car yesterday.	They crash(ed) the car yesterday.
I wash my hands before I have lunch.	I wash my hands before I have lunch.
I washed my hands before I had lunch.	I wash(ed) my hands before I had lunch.
They usually finish their work at six.	They usually finish their work at six.
They finished work early yesterday.	They finish(ed) work early yesterday.

3 Even the negative <-t> may disappear at speed. For example:

slow version	fast version
I can't say	I can('t) say
I don't know	I don('t) know
Can't pay, won't pay.	Can('t) pay, won('t) pay.
They haven't finished work.	They haven('t) finish(ed) work.

4 Because of /d/ or /t/ elision a number of different words, when spoken at speed, can sound exactly the same. For example:

slow version	fast version
We need the facts today	We need the fac(t)s today = We need the fax today
I just saw the prints	I jus(t) saw the prin(t)s = I just saw the prince
Have you heard about the finds?	Have you heard about the fin(d)s = Have you heard about the fines?
Please buy some mints	Please buy some min(t)s = Please buy some mince
Cold storage	Col(d) storage = Coal storage
fast food	fas(t) food = farce food

Note that /t/ has a tendency to disappear even when it is not between two consonants. *Let's go* can be les gəʊ, sounding like *less go*, for example.

Task twenty-five

Here are various compounds and phrases. In most of them elision of /d/ or /t/ is possible. See how quickly you can identify the ones where it is **not** possible.

software	compact disc	hardware
landmine	postman	loud speaker
sound check	stand by	child birth
handcuffs	smart card	wild fire
word perfect	old boy	best man
sandbag	east bound	turned off

A2 Elision of identical or similar consonants

a) Identical consonants

Concentrate on the final consonants in the following words:

lamp = /læmp/   six = /sɪks/

prime = /praɪm/   lettuce = /letəs/

Now see what tends to happen when these words are followed by another word starting with the same consonant.

very slow version	normal version
a lamp post = ə ˈlæmp ˌpəʊst	(sounds like) a lamb post = ə ˈlæm ˌpəʊst
six students = ˌsɪks ˈstjuːdənts	(sounds like) sick students = ˌsɪk ˈstjuːdns
Prime Minister = ˌpraɪm ˈmɪnɪstə	(sounds like) pry minister = ˌpraɪ ˈmɪnɪstə
lettuce salad = ˌletəs ˈsæləd	(sounds like) letter salad = ˌletə ˈsæləd

When two identical consonants meet, as in the above examples, then you are unlikely to produce both of them. And this is not limited to fast speech; even BBC newsreaders refer to the Prime Minister as the *pry minister*. (Check what *pry* means and you'll see why that amuses me.)

Again it is a question of saving yourself effort. Take *lamp post*; in order to produce /p/ you have to: close your lips; gather air behind the place of closure; open the glottis (or it will sound like /b/); then release the lips. And to say / ˈlæmp ˌpəʊst/ you have to do this twice in rapid sequence. So what happens in the case of plosives, such as /p/, is that you do it just the once.

With continuants (as in *Prime Minister*) the sound is lengthened slightly. Imagine it as *Prymmminister*.

b) Similar consonants

The above examples concerned the coming together of **identical** consonants. But it also happens with what we can think of as **similar** consonants. This is not a technical term, but I use it to refer to sounds which are produced at or about the same point in the mouth: such as those found at the start of the following words: *dog* = dɒg; *table* = teɪbl; *chicken* = tʃɪkɪn; and *jar* = dʒɑː.

All of them are produced with the tongue making contact at more or less the same point: at or just behind the teeth-ridge. So it saves time, when these sounds meet, if the release of air is only made after the second has been produced. Thus *fried chicken*, instead of being pronounced /ˌfraɪd ˈtʃɪkɪn/, tends to sound like *fry chicken*, since the /d/ becomes part of the /tʃ/ of *chicken*.

Listen to the following, involving both identical and similar consonants.

very slow version	fast version	very slow version	fast version
a dark curl	a dar(k) curl	hard judges	har(d) judges
a dark girl	a dar(k) girl	soap powder	soa(p) powder
a good dog	a goo(d) dog	soap bowl	soa(p) bowl
a good time	a goo(d) time	this singer	thi(s) singer
a big girl	a bi(g) girl	these singers	the(se) singers
a big cake	a bi(g) cake		

Note: This type of elision can affect grammatical sequences, too.

For example, the sequence *used to* (*When I was young I used to live in Brighton*) is only pronounced /juːst tuː/ when one is speaking very, very slowly. Normally it is pronounced /juːstə/, as if it were *use to*.

And the reduced form of *had* in a sentence such as, *I'd just got in when the phone rang*, normally becomes so much part of the following *just* that the sequence sounds exactly like *I just got in when the phone rang*.

A3 elision of initial consonants in pronouns

In Part 1 we talked about strong and weak forms of pronouns. Listen again to part of an earlier poem, paying particular attention to the pronunciation of the pronoun *he*.

1 The first boy said that he'd like a slice of bread.
2 The second boy muttered that he'd really like it buttered.
3 The third boy replied that he'd rather have it fried.
4 The next boy trilled that he much preferred it grilled.
5 The last boy was quiet ... but *he* was on a diet.

What happens is that in lines 1 to 4 the pronoun *he* is unimportant and unstressed. So, when spoken at this speed, it loses the initial /h/ sound and becomes a simple /i/, linked to the preceding *that*.

Now listen to line 5. In this case the pronoun *he* has its full, strong form /hiː/. This is because he, the last boy, contrasts with the other four. So, the pronoun *he* is found in this poem in two distinct forms:

● /i/, the very **weak, unstressed** form; and

● /hiː/, the **strong, stressed** form.

Other pronouns in their weakest forms may also lose their initial consonants. You can practise three of them, *her*, *him* and *them*, in the following chant, 'Have you seen Peter?' Note that the chant also gives practice in contrasting the use of the past simple and present perfect tenses. Compare:

past simple	present perfect
I saw him half an hour ago.	I've just seen her talking.
I saw them Tuesday morning.	I've seen him fairly frequently.
I saw her several hours ago.	I haven't seen her since Christmas.
I glimpsed him in the canteen.	I've seen her several times today.

Remember that the **past simple** is associated with specific moments in the past: *half an hour ago / Tuesday morning / (when I was) in the canteen*. The **present perfect**, by contrast, refers to an unspecified time or a time extending up to the present – *fairly frequently / since Christmas / several times today* – and may be found in the context *I've just ...*

Have you seen Peter? (1)

1 Have you seen Peter? Have you seen Pete?
   I saw (h)im half an hour ago, running down the street.

2 Have you seen Patricia, have you seen Pat?
   I've just seen (h)er talking to ᵂ(h)er little ginger cat.

3 Have you seen my neighbours, Anthony and Mark?
   I saw (th)em Tuesday morning, strolling in the park.

4 Have you seen Samantha, have you seen Sam?
   I saw (h)er several hours ago, eating bread and jam.

5 Have you seen Vincent, have you seen Vince?
   I talked to ᵂ(h)im on Tuesday, but I haven't seen him since

6 Have you seen William, have you seen Bill?
   I may have seen (h)im yesterday, walking up the hill.

7 Have you seen Benjamin, have you seen Ben?
   I've seen (h)im somewhere recently, I can't remember when.

8 Have you seen Violet, have you seen Vi?
   I spoke to (h)er this morning, but I can't remember why.

9 Have you seen Matthew, have you seen Mat?
   I saw (h)im talking to the Queen, so what do you think of that!

10 Have you seen Susan, have you seen Sue?
   I haven'(t) seen (h)er since Christmas and I don't know what to do!

Have you seen Peter? (2)

Task twenty-six

In the second version of the chant the second line ends with a missing one-syllable adjective. See if you can guess the word. If not, choose it from the list on page 74. As you can see from the example, more than one may be possible. (Note that we have put in some words that cannot fit.)

1 Have you seen Peter, have you seen Pete?
   I spotted (h)im an hour ago, looking very (neat / sweet)

2 Have you seen my parents, my mum and my dad?
   I've seen (th)em several times today, looking really (...................)

3 Have you seen Nelly, have you seen Nell?
   I saw (h)er in the classroom, looking very (...................)

4 Have you seen my parents, my dad and my mum?
   I 've seen (th)em once or twice today , looking pretty (...................)

5 Have you seen Patrick, have you seen Pat?
  I glimpsed (h)im in the canteen, looking very (....................)

6 Have you seen Nicholas, have you seen Nick?
  I saw (h)im in the cinema, looking slightly (....................)

7 Have you seen my cousins, Anthony and Bart?
  I noticed (th)em a while ago, looking rather (....................)

8 Have you seen Diana, have you seen Di?
  I've seen (h)er once or twice today, looking rather (....................)

9 Have you seen Jimmy, have you seen Jim?
  I saw (h)im twenty minutes back, looking very (....................)

10 Have you seen Lynda, have you seen Lyn?
   I've seen (h)er several times today, looking very (....................)

11 Have you seen Katie, have you seen Kate?
   I've see (h)er twice this afternoon, looking really (....................)

12 Have you seen what's-his-name, the man from number nine?
   I saw (h)im down the pub last night, looking really (....................)

13 Have you seen what's-her-name, the girl from number two?
   I think I've seen (h)er recently, looking very (....................)

---

blue / numb / late / grim / bad / thin / sick / hell / thick / glum / glad /
high / swell / mad / flat / new / shy / fat / sad / great / fine / tart /
quick / nine / smart / slim / mine / well / sly

B Anticipatory assimilation

assimilation of /n/

We have already come across this form of assimilation, where the nasal consonant /n/ can change to become more like the following sound. In Part 1 we said:

'In *and Patricia*, for example, the /d/ goes and then the /n/ becomes /m/ because of the following /p/ and we end up with əm pə'trɪʃə. In the same way, *and Kate* = əŋ 'keit.(The symbol /ŋ/ represents the consonant sound at the end of *song*, *thing*, *wrong* etc.)'

We saw the same thing happening with *the secon(d) boy* and *the seco(n)d girl*.

- *secon(d) boy* became /sekəm bɔɪ/, the /d/ being elided and the /n/ changing to /m/ because of the following /b/.

- *seco(n)d girl* became /sekəŋ gɜːl/, the /d/ again going, but this time the /n/ changing to /ŋ/ because of the following /g/.

Task twenty-seven

Read the following poem aloud and see if you can work out:

● when the letter <n> in the word *ten* will still be pronounced /n/ even when read quite fast, and

● when the /n/ will change to something else.

● Then listen to the tape and see if you were right.

Ten boys and ten girls

1 Ten boys and ten girls; ten rubies, ten pearls.	5 Ten peaches, ten grapes; ten monkeys, ten apes.
2 Ten dogs and ten cats; ten coats and ten hats.	6 Ten brooches, ten rings; ten people, ten things.
3 Ten pounds and ten marks; ten gardens, ten parks.	7 Ten saucers, ten cups; Ten downs and ten ups.
4 Ten shouts and ten sighs; ten truths and ten lies.	8 Ten dolls and ten toys; ten girls and ten boys.

As usual, it is a question of making things easy for the speaker. If you are going to close your lips for /b/ or /p/, say, then it is easier to close them for the preceding nasal. Similarly, if you are going to produce a nasal before raising the back of the tongue to the soft palate, it might as well be the nasal which belongs there anyway.

assimilation of /d/ and /t/

In addition to /n/, the other two alveolar consonants /d/ and /t/ can also assimilate.

/d/ can become:

● /b/ (before /b/ or /p/), or

● /g/ (before /g/ or /k/), so

sequence	slow version	fast version
third boy	θɜːd bɔɪ	θɜːb bɔɪ
third person	θɜːd pɜːsən	θɜːb pɜːsən
third girl	θɜːd gɜːl	θɜːg gɜːl
third cat	θɜːd kæt	θɜːg kæt

/t/ can become

● /p/ (before /b/ or /p/), or

● /k/ (before /g/ or /k/)

But, rather more commonly, /t/ can become a **glottal stop** before another consonant, even another /t/. For example:

sequence	slow version	fast version	or
that boy	ðæt bɔɪ	ðæp bɔɪ	ðæʔ bɔɪ
that person	ðæt pɜːsən	ðæp pɜːsən	ðæʔ pɜːsən
that girl	ðæt ɡɜːl	ðæk ɡɜːl	ðæʔ ɡɜːl
that cat	ðæt kæt	ðæk kæt	ðæʔ kæt
that time	ðæt taɪm		ðæʔ taɪm

elision giving rise to assimilation

In sequences such as *ten boys* and *ten girls* assimilation takes place because the sounds involved are already next to each other.

By contrast, in others such as *the second boy* and *the second girl* assimilation only takes place because the intervening sound – the /d/ in this case – has been elided.

There are hundreds of set expressions involving this combination of /d/ or /t/ elision + assimilation.

Using 'and'

eggs an(d) bacon	/ˌeɡzəm ˈbeɪkən/
boys an(d) girls	/ˌbɔɪzəŋ ˈɡɜːlz/
tea an(d) coffee	/ˌtiːʲəŋ ˈkɒfi/
en(d)s an(d) means	/ˌenzəm ˈmiːnz/

negative /t/

I won('t) be coming	/aɪ ˌwəʊm bi ˈkʌmɪŋ/
She can('t) go	/ʃi ˈkɑːŋ ˈɡəʊ/
Can('t) pay, won('t) pay	/ˌkɑːmpeɪ ˈwəʊmpeɪ/
I don('t) care	/aɪ ˌdəʊŋ ˈkeə/

compounds and phrases

Here is a small selection of dozens of compounds and phrases where assimilation occurs: *lan(d) mine / ren(t) book / gran(d)mother / han(d)cuffs / han(d)bag / win(d)mill / san(d)bag / sal(t) mine / stan(d) back / corn(ed) beef / tinn(ed) beans / sal(t) beef* etc.

And you do not have to speak at all fast for such assimilation to take place. The word *handcuffs* sounds as if it were *hangcuffs* more often than not; and your *grandmother* is usually your *grammother*.

The importance of collocation and frequency of use

In fact speed of delivery, the rate at which you speak, is only one factor in deciding whether elision and/or assimilation is likely to take place; there are two further factors which come into play.

The first is **collocation**. By this we mean, the frequency with which words (or other elements) are found together. Thus the items *compact + disc* are more likely to be found together (i.e. to **collocate**) than *compact + bathroom* or *warped + disc*, say. Hence the /t/ in *compact disc* is more likely to be elided than that in the two other phrases.

The second is **frequency of use**. When compact discs were a rarity, people presumably used the phrase *compact disc* quite carefully, unsure that other people would be familiar with the expression. But as the things became more familiar, so the name became used more frequently and would be spoken with greater ease and rapidity.

Take the word *handkerchief*. It used to be composed of two separate words: *hand + kerchief*. But they became so closely associated in the compound *handkerchief* that the /d/ disppeared permanently; it is incorrect to pronounce the /d/ nowadays.

In *handbag* the /d/, by contrast, has not permanently disappeared. But you would have to be speaking very slowly and emphatically to pronounce it.

When you come to a much less common compound – *handmaid*, for example, – you are much more likely to pronounce the full word, /d/ included.

So we can establish the useful principle that the more frequently two elements come together (= the greater their likelihood of collocation), the more probable it is that a change will occur.

Task twenty-eight

This task is to see if you can identify elision and assimilation. There is quite a lot of both in the following poem: *Born and bred in London*. For example, the /t/ or /d/ of final -*ed* disappears in a number of cases: listen out for:

I've jogg(ed) down … stroll(ed) through … saunter(ed) down … walk(ed) the … lurch(ed) down.

But elision and/or assimilation can also occur where two words meet in place-names. *Wood Green* can become /ˌwʊɡ ˈɡriːn/, for example, and *Green Park* /ˌɡriːm ˈpɑːk/.

In this poem there is one (and only one) example in each verse of a place name being affected by elision and/or assimilation. So:

● Read the poem to yourself and try to predict which place name in each verse is changed because of assimilation.

● Listen to it several times to see if you can hear it happening.

(Don't worry too much about the meaning of the different verbs; we'll deal with this in the next task.)

Born and bred in London

I was born and bred in London;
I know it like the back of my hand;
from Camden Lock
to the Shell-Mex clock,
from Old Street to the Strand.

I've jogged down Piccadilly
and strolled through Leicester Square,
been to Holland Park
for a ramble in the dark,
and to Hampstead for the fair.

I know every street in London;
I could do it with my eyes tight shut;
from Madame Tussauds
to the House of Lords
From Hyde Park to The Cut.

I've sauntered down to Kentish Town
and run to Tottenham Hale,
walked the Old Kent Road
while it hailed and snowed
and lurched down Maida Vale.

I know my way round London,
no-one knows it better than me;
been to Hammersmith Palais,
Covent Garden for the ballet
and The Ritz for china tea.

I visit the Bond Street Galleries,
I'm seen at the best affairs;
go to Waterloo
for a private view,
drink Pimm's on the Crush Bar stairs.

I've been everywhere in London,
by taxi, bus and train;
I've crawled, I've biked,
I've hopped, I've hiked,
from Saint Paul's to Drury Lane.

And though I've seen the lot now,
from London Bridge to Kew,
I would do it all again,
From Blackheath to old Big Ben,
just to show it all to you.

Note that names with *Street* are compounds: OLD street, OXford Street, BOND Street etc. All other two-part place names are phrases:

‚Oxford 'Circus, ‚Hyde 'Park, ‚London 'Bridge, ‚Saint 'Paul's etc.

Task twenty-nine

The poem is full of verbs of movement. Use your dictionary, if necessary, to check the meanings, then put ticks in the appropriate squares to complete the grid.

	on hands and knees	faster than walking	on one foot	no sense of hurry	usually in the country	out of control
jog						
stroll						
ramble						
saunter						
run						
lurch						
crawl						
hop						
hike						

Task thirty

A diner is a type of restaurant best-known in the USA. (You may have seen them in films from the 50s and 60s.) They usually have a long counter with a row of single stools, and a few booths for four people from where you can choose music from the juke-box. I wrote this rap after eating in a genuine restored original diner here in London, 'Fatboy's Diner', situated between Covent Garden and the Strand.

Your task this time is a dictatation. All the names of things to eat or drink have been cut out. Listen to the rap as often as you want to, and fill in all the gaps bit by bit. This is quite fast (but no faster than regular informal speech), so watch out for elision and assimilation, especially where an *-ed* may disappear between two consonants.

Down the diner

I was sitting down the diner, toying with my food,
looking at the papers, in a lazy kind of mood

when a little skinny fellow I'd never seen before
came and sat down beside me, and this is what I saw:

my favourite waitress, Sally, came over to the guy
to ask him for his order, and this was his reply:

'I'd like a (1) .... , make sure it's really hot,
and a (2) .... should really hit the spot,

with a (3) .... and a touch of (4) ....
then a (5) .... with some (6) .... and (7) .... ,

and a (8) .... or two of (9) .... with some (10) ....
then a (11) .... , with some (12) .... of course.

Can I have the (13) .... in a (14) .... ?
and a good thick (15) .... well-done;

and how about some (16) .... , I like them lightly fried,
with a little piccalilli and some (17) .... on the side

and I'd like to try a couple of your (18) .... pies.
with a pile of (19) .... and a plate of (20) ....

then a (21) .... – cut it really thick,
with a little (22) .... , now that should do the trick.

For dessert I think I'll start with a good old (23) ....
with several (24) .... of (25) .... , pile 'em really high;

then a (26) .... of little (27) .... with some (28) .... on top
and an (29) .... ; perhaps I'd better stop.

No, maybe there's some (30) .... that you can recommend?
OK I'll take the (31) .... and that'll be the end.'

So Sally took the order though she thought it was a joke,
then the fellow called her back and said,

'I'd like (32) .... '

Task thirty-one

Here is another poem full of examples of **assimilation** and **elision**. Don't listen to it yet. Just read it through carefully and see if you can guess which of the following words and phrases will involve elision and/or assimilation.

best friend	another friend	twenty pounds
landlord	sandwiches	one editor
another one	next door	brand-new
beef hash	a third one	second-hand

Task thirty-two

Now listen to the poem and see if you can note down every example of elision and assimilation.

> **Vocabulary notes**
> a fortnight *back* = 'a fortnight ago/ two weeks ago';
> *corned-beef* is a type of tinned beef;
> *dosh* is a slang word for 'cash', 'money';
> a *hash* is usually made with meat, potatoes etc. all mixed together and cooked;
> *mack* is short for *mackintosh* = 'rain-coat' (note: a 'Mac' is an Apple Mackintosh computer);
> to *sneak away* is to leave quietly so that nobody can see you leaving;
> *tosh* means 'nonsense', 'rubbish', 'of no value'.

Cash-flow problems

My best friend bought me
a brand-new hand-bag;
another friend bought me
a second-hand mack;
My next door neighbour
said he'd lend me
twenty pounds till Monday.
      The problem is
          I don't know how
               I'm going to pay them back!

My landlord brought me
some roast-beef sandwiches;
my landlady made me
some corned-beef hash;
my grandmother sent me
a case of canned potatoes.
      The problem is
          I don't know where
               I'm going to get the cash!

One editor said that
she rather liked a poem;
another one said that
they were a load of tosh;
a third one said that
they might use one at Christmas.
　　　　The problem is
　　　　　　it's right now
　　　　　　　　I really need
　　　　　　　　　　the dosh!

A fortnight back I told them all
I'd come up with the money.
Last week I promised that
I'd really, truly pay.
If I haven't got it next week
there's only one thing for it.
　　　　I'd better get
　　　　　　my bags
　　　　　　　　all packed
　　　　　　　　　and quietly
　　　　　　　　　　　sneak
　　　　　　　　　　　　away.

Coalescent assimilation

1 /d/ or /t/ + /j/

The last poem 'Cash flow problems' contained the line *they might use one at Christmas*. Spoken slowly and carefully this would be:

ðeɪ maɪt juːz wʌn ət krɪsməs

But *might* ends with a /t/ and *use* begins with a /j/. And the sound /j/ tends to combine with a preceding /d/ or /t/. The formula is:

● /t/ + /j/ may coalesce to become /tʃ/ (= the first sound in *child*, *Charles* etc.)

● /d/ + /j/ may coalesce to become /dʒ/ (= the first sound in *jam*, *Jane* etc.)

So the sequence *might use*, at normal fast speed, will sound like *my choose*.

This type of assimilation is particularly important because it involves some combinations of words which are so common that coalescence happens extremely frequently in ordinary speech.

a) /t/ + /j/

1 An extremely common context for /t/ to meet /j/ is when the short version of *not* is followed by *you* or *your*.

sequence	slow version	fast version
can't you?	kɑːnt juː	kɑːntʃə
won't you?	wəʊnt juː	wəʊntʃə
don't you?	dəʊnt juː	dəʊntʃə
Can't you come?	kɑːnt juː kʌm	kɑːntʃə kʌm
didn't you?	dɪdnt juː	dɪdntʃə
Didn't your (mother do it?)	dɪdnt jɔː	dɪdntʃə
wouldn't you?	wʊdnt juː	wʊdntʃə
Wouldn't your (friends help?)	wʊdnt jɔː	wʊdntʃə

2 Another context is when a stressed verb ending in /t/ is followed by *you* or *your*.

I **bet you** can't do it.	aɪ 'betʃə 'kɑːn 'duː ʷɪt
I'll **meet your** friend tomorrow.	aɪl 'miːtʃə 'fren tə'mɒrəʊ
I can't **let you** do it.	aɪ 'kɑːn letʃə 'duː ʷɪt [1]
I'll **treat your** friends (to the cinema).	aɪl 'triːtʃə 'frenz
I **admit you** were right.	aɪ ədmɪtʃʊ wə 'raɪt

3 Similar coalescence can take place when the sound /t/, functioning as the <-ed> suffix, is followed by *you* or *your*. For example:

I **picked your** book up.	aɪ 'pɪktʃə 'bʊ kʌp
We **stopped you** from doing it.	wi 'stɒptʃə frəm 'dəʊɪŋ ɪt

Note that this form of assimilation can take place even with stressed *you* or *your*. So, *Don't YOU want it?* can sound like *Don('t) CHEW want it?*

b) /d/ + /j/

1 Probably the most frequent cause of /d/ + /j/ assimilation is when certain auxiliary or modal verbs meet *you*.

These are not only those verbs – *did*, *could* and *would* – which always end in /d/, but also the weakest form of *do*, where the vowel disappears completely.

At this point we need to mention again that there are not always just two possibilities – a slow version and a fast one. Listen to three versions of the following four sequences:

---

1 Note that *let you* and *let your* sound the same as *lecher* when spoken fast; and *picked you/picked your* sound like *picture*.

a) Do you like jazz?

slow = duː juː ˈlaɪk ˈdʒæz
fast = dʊ jʊ ˈlaɪk ˈdʒæz
very fast = dʒə ˈlaɪk ˈdʒæz

b) Did you like the music?

slow = dɪd juː ˈlaɪk ðə ˈmjuːzik
fast = dɪdʒə ˈlaɪk ðə ˈmjuːzik
very fast = dʒə ˈlaɪk ðə ˈmjuːzik

c) Would you like to go again?

slow = wʊd juː ˈlaɪk tə ˈɡəʊ əˈɡen
fast = wʊdʒə ˈlaɪk tə ˈɡəʊ əˈɡen
very fast = dʒə ˈlaɪk tə ˈɡəʊ əˈɡen

d) Did you have a good time?

slow = dɪd juː ˈhæv ə ˈɡʊd ˈtaɪm
fast = dɪd ˈjæv ə ˈɡʊd ˈtaɪm
very fast = ˈdʒæv ə ˈɡʊd ˈtaɪm

So, in very fast casual speech there need be no difference at all between *do you*, *did you* and *would you*; they can all be pronounced dʒə. When I tell this to students they sometimes ask how we can tell the difference. The answer is that the context always makes it clear. Listen to the following questions and answers, which also show the difference between the weakest and strongest forms of the auxiliaries.

Do you like jazz?	Yes, I do.
dʒə ˈlaɪk ˈdʒæz	je saɪ ˈduː
Did you like the music last night?	Yes, I did.
dʒə ˈlaɪk ðə ˈmjuːzik ˈlɑːs ˈnaɪt	je saɪ ˈdɪd
Would you like to go again ?	Yes, I would.
dʒə ˈlaɪk tə ˈɡəʊ ə ˈgen	je saɪ ˈwʊd

2 verbs ending in /d/ followed by *you* / *your*

I've **made your** bed.	aɪv ˈmeɪdʒə ˈbed
Have you **paid your** bill?	həv jə ˈpeɪdʒə ˈbɪl
I **said you** should come.	aɪ ˈsedʒə ʃʊɡ ˈkʌm

Note that as with /t/ the assimilation can take place even with the stressed forms of *you* and *your*.

3   -ed

I **mentioned your** name.	aɪ ˈmenʃəndʒə ˈneɪm
I **wanted you** to come.	aɪ ˈwʌntɪdʒə tə ˈkʌm
They **said you** shouldn(ʻt) do it.	ðeɪ ˈsedʒʊ ˈʃʊdn ˈduː ʷɪt

Now practice this form of assimilation by listening to and repeating the 'Chinatown' rap. On the left of the page it is written to give an idea of the pronunciation, with the letter <a> representing schwa.

normal form	written here	phonetic notation
want to	wanna	ˈwʌnə
going to	goinTa	ˈɡəʊɪntə
do you	dja	dʒə
what do you	whatcha	ˈwɒtʃə
don't you	dontcha	ˈdəʊntʃə
let you	letcha	ˈletʃə
couldn't you	couldntcha	ˈkʊdntʃə
have to	hafta[2]	ˈhæftə
did you	didja	ˈdɪdʒə
how did you	howdja	ˈhaʊdʒə
where do you	wheredja	ˈweədʒə
lots of	lotsa	ˈlɒtsə
the name of	the namea	ðə ˈneɪmə
a bit of	a bit a	ə ˈbɪtə
sure to	sure ta	ˈʃɔːtə

Other features of fast speech are also reflected in the changes of spelling. Look out for:

elision/lengthening of identical/similar sounds	
Normal form	written here
I'm not too sure	I'm no' too sure
I'll leave it to you	I' leave it to you
I'll let you know	I' letcha know
It's sure to please	It' sure ta please

elision of /t/	
Normal form	written here
Let's just meet	Le's just meet
didn't say	didn' say
I don't know	I don' know
it wasn't written	it wasn' written

---

2   This spelling of *have to* shows how, at speed, the /v/ of *have* can become /f/, losing its voicing to be more like the following /t/ sound.

Important note:

Don't get so carried away by the rhythm that you read the rap like a machine. Remember that language has music, too.

Listen, listen, listen, many, many times, thinking how the voice goes up and down. DAH du DAH it before you say the words. And when you finally rap it along with the tape, follow the voices up and down.

Don't forget that the pitch changes (how we go from high to low, from low to high) are smoooooooooth on the stressed syllables. Take the title word, *Chinatown*. We don't say it in three equal stages, as if it were:

          Chi

                    na

                          town

Instead, there is a nice smooth, steady fall on *Chi*, with the next two syllables safe at the bottom of the voice, not moving. So think of it as:

C h
   i.
     i.
       i na town

Finally, remember that this is a conversation. It may sound fast, but it is no faster than regular, informal speech.

But don't think you have to repeat it all at once. You can practice a sequence in short bits, starting from the end to keep the intonation going.

Try it with the following sentences.

1 a show?
   see a show?
   ta see a show?
   ta town ta see a show?
   go ta town ta see a show?
   wanna go ta town ta see a show?
   Doncha wanna go ta town ta see a show?

2 Chinatown?
   in Chinatown?
   first in Chinatown?
   fancy eating first in Chinatown?
   Dja fancy eating first in Chinatown?

Chinatown

How it sounds	How it is written
A: Where dja wanna go ? **Whatcha** wanna do ?	Where do you want to go ? What do you want to do ?
B: I'm **no'** too sure, I' **leave** it ta you.	I'm not too sure, I'll leave it to you.
A: Doncha wanna go ta town ta **see** a show ?	Don't you want to go to town to see a show ?
B: I **don'** know now, but I' **let**cha know.	I don't know now, but I'll let you know.
A: Couldntcha tell me **right** away ?	Couldn't you tell me right away?
B: I'm **not** sure yet. Do I **haf**ta say?	I'm not sure yet. Do I have to say?
A: Where dja wanna meet ? Wontcha **tell** me where ?	Where do you want to meet ? Won't you tell me where ?
B: Le's jus' meet in **Leic**ester Square.	Let's just meet in Leicester Square.
A: Didja tell the others where we're **go**inta meet ?	Did you tell the others where we're going to meet ?
B: I **said** in the centre, didn' **say** which street.	I said in the centre, didn't say which street.
A: Dja **wan**na have a meal or dja **like** ta sit down ?	Do you want to have a meal or would you like to sit down?
B: Dja **fan**cy eating first in **Chi**natown?	Do you fancy eating first in Chinatown?
A: Whatcha recommend ? Wheredja **like** ta dine?	What do you recommend? Where would you like to dine ?
B: Here's very good, their **fish** is fine.	Here's very good, their fish is fine.
A: How's the fish cooked, with **lots**a spice?	How's the fish cooked, with lots of spice?
B: Just a bit a ginger, it's **real**ly nice.	Just a bit of ginger, it's really nice.
A: Whatcha like ta drink when you **eat** Chinese?	What do you like to drink when you eat Chinese?

B: **Just** a pot a tea,	Just a pot of tea,
it' **sure** ta please.	it's sure to please.
A: **How**dja like the meal,	How did you like the meal,
Didja **like** the fish ?	Did you like the fish ?
B: It was **real**ly great,	It was really great,
what's the **name**a the dish?	What's the name of the dish?
A: I **don**' know the name;	I don't know the name;
it **was**n' written down.	it wasn't written down.
B: That's **of**ten the way	That's often the way
... in **Chi**natown.	... in Chinatown.

3 /s/ or /z/ + /j/

The fricatives /s/ and /z/ can also coalesce with /j/.

- /s/ + /j/ → /ʃ/ (as in *shop*, *she*, *ship*, *dish* etc.)

- /z/ + /j/ → /ʒ/ (as in *pleasure*, *television*, *camouflage* etc.)

sequence	slow version	fast version
Is this yours?	ɪz ðɪs ˈjɔːz	ɪz ðɪ ˈʃɔːz
Yes, you can.	jes juː ˈkæn	jeʃə ˈkæn
He's your brother.	hiːz jɔː ˈbrʌðə	hiːʒə ˈbrʌðə
Are these yours?	ɑː ðiːz ˈjɔːz	ɑː ðiː ˈʒɔːz

Task thirty-three

Listen to the chant on the next page while reading the text. Pay special attention to what happens to the /j/ sound in *you*, *your* and *yourself* when the teacher replies.

Here are the words that come before *you*, *your* and *yourself*. Each ends in either /s/ or /z/. Tick the appropriate column.

	/s/	/z/		/s/	/z/
course			please		
discuss			express		
miss			revise		
use			pass		
practise			amaze		

Can I ask you something?

Student	Teacher
1 Can I ask you something?	Of course you can.
2 It's all so hard.	Let's discuss your problems.
3 I'm falling behind.	Don't miss your lessons.
4 I don't understand.	Well, use your head.
5 My accent's bad.	Well, practise your pron.
6 Should I listen to some tapes?	Please yourself.
7 I don't know what to write.	Just express yourself.
8 I make lots of mistakes.	Revise your grammar.
9 How d'you think I'll do?	You're sure to pass your exam.
10 Do you really think I will?	You'll amaze your friends.

Rapping the rules

These first three parts have covered the main features of spoken English, in terms of rhythm and stress. These are summarised in a set of five rules which I've written as a rap. The five rules are:

1   You have to stress the correct syllables. And the weak syllables must **never** be too long. The schwa, in particular, is very short.
Remember that placing main stress in the wrong place is the best way for people not to understand you.

2   To keep the rhythm flowing along you have to link individual words. Remember:

one napple, two wapples, three yapples, four rapples

3   And it's much easier if you elide the sounds that native speakers do, especially the /d/ and /t/ between consonants.

4   Natural speech also means that we can make it easier to pass from one sound to the next by changing the first to be more like the second (i.e. anticipatory assimilation).

5   Finally, two sounds may join together to become one, especially when /d/, /t/, /s/ and /ʃ/meet /j/ (i.e coalescent assimilation).

Rapping the rules

If you **want** to make your **Eng**lish **come alive**,
just **lis**ten to my **rules** from **one** to **five**.

1   If you **don't** want your **Eng**lish to **sound** a **mess**,
you've **got** to hit the **beat**, you've **got** to hit the **stress**.
But you're **go**ing to sound **fun**ny, it's **go**ing to go **wrong**
if you **make** your **weak** sounds **much** too **strong**.

2 And **words** go to**ge**ther like **links** in a **chain**;
they **fol**low ea**ch o**ther like **wag**gons on a **train**.

3 Now **lis**ten really **close** and **you** will **hear**
that **cer**tain kinds of **sound** can **dis**appear.

4 And re**mem**ber if you **want** to in**crease** your **range**
that a **sound** can **make** a**noth**er sound **change**.

5 You're **get**ting better **now**, but to **be** the **best**,
just re**mem**ber two **sounds** can **coalesce**.

You've **got** five **sens**es, you've **got** five **rules**,
so **use** them **all** and you **won't** be **fools**.
So, to **make** your **Eng**lish **buzz** like a **hive**,
just **think** of **one, two, three, four, FIVE!**

Task thirty-four

The last task in this part of the book is like a final examination to see how good your ear has become. What you have to do is listen to the rap very carefully in order to see how the rules apply when you speak at this speed. (And remember this: the rap might sound fast, but it's no faster than regular, informal spoken English.)

So go through the text and note:

a) every example of **linking** in Verse 2;

b) every example of **elision** in the introduction and Verse 5;

c) every example of **anticipatory assimilation** in Verses 3, 4 and 5;

d) every example of **coalescent assimilation** in the whole rap.

In the first three parts of the book you have leaned a lot about what happens in spoken English.

The rest of the book is to help you put your new skills into practice.

Part 4

PART 4

PLAYING WITH POEMS

Introduction

In this part there are a number of poems which have been chosen for two reasons:

● to give you practice in the rhythm of spoken English, and

● to improve and increase your vocabulary.

The tasks in this section are of various types. Most involve filling gaps with appropriate words; in others you will have to match parts of sentences, do some rewriting, and so on.

All the limericks have been recorded, so you can listen to the tape to help you with the task or after completing it.

Whatever the task, remember that the choice of words depends on two things: firstly, the **meaning**, obviously; a word has to make sense, to fit into the rest of the text; but as these texts are poems, it also has to fit the **metre** (i.e. the beat, the rhythm) and, if the word is at the end of a line, it has to fit the **rhyme scheme** too.

Feel free to listen to the poems before trying the tasks, if you feel happier. And if you are wondering which word fits a gap, try the DAH du du technique; this will help you to work out if you need a word with one syllable, or two or three. If it is a 2-syllable word, it will help you decide if the pattern is ○ ■ or ■ ○, for example.

Remember, once more, not to worry too much if you do not understand 100%. Concentrate on the rhythm and music; imagine the words flowing by like waves on the sea and follow them along, with all their up and down movements. Poems are to be enjoyed, not to be worried about.

A LIMERICKS

A1 What are limericks?

Limericks are very simple poems. Listen to the following, very typical one.

> **A:** There once was a person from Lyme
> **A:** who married three wives at a time.
> **B:** When asked 'Why a third?'
> **B:** He replied, 'One's absurd!
> **A:** And bigamy, sir, is a crime!'

Like all limericks it has the following characteristics.

● It consists of **five lines**.

● The **rhyme scheme** is A A B B A.
  This means that lines 1, 2 and 5 have one rhyme (in this case *Lyme / time / crime*), while lines 3 and 4 have a different rhyme (in this case *third / absurd*).

● The **metre** (or beat) is as regular as the rhyme scheme: three beats in the A line, and two in the B lines. Listen again while beating it out.

>   a   ONE   and a   TWO and a   THREE
> **A:** There once was a person from Lyme
>
>   a   ONE   and a   TWO and a THREE
> **A:** who married three wives at a time.
>
>   a   ONE   and a   TWO
> **B:** When asked 'Why a third?'
>
>   a   ONE   and a   TWO
> **B:** He replied, 'One's absurd!
>
>   a ONE and a TWO and a THREE
> **A:** And bigamy, sir, is a crime!'

Note also that the first line refers to a person from a particular place. This is not obligatory, but many limericks have a similar reference in the first line.

> When doing the tasks in this section, it is a good idea to have a good dictionary handy, so that you can check the rhymes (as well as the meanings).

A2 Gap-fill tasks

Task thirty-five
The rhyming words in the following limerick have been jumbled together at the end. Fill them in as quickly as you can

> 1 There once was an old man from ...
> 2 who dreamed he was eating his ...
> 3 He woke up in the ...
> 4 with a terrible ...
> 5 and found it was perfectly ...

> fright / shoe / true / night / Crewe

Task thirty-six
Here are two limericks on the theme of music, with their rhyming words jumbled up at the end. Again fill them as quickly as possible.

> 1 A musician who came from Hong ...
> 2 Composed a new popular ...
> 3 But the song that he ...
> 4 Was all on one ...
> 5 Though it sounded superb on a ...

 6 A musical girl called ...
 7 Played 'God Save the Queen' on a ...
 8 Or so she ...
 9 But people who ...
10 Were never quite able to ...

tell / wrote / Kong / heard / song / Estelle /
averred (= said, stated, claimed) / bell / gong / note

Task thirty-seven

And now we go up to three limericks with the rhyming words left out and jumbled
up. And this time an extra word has been added for each rhyme, to confuse things.

 1 A diner while dining at ...
 2 Found a rather large mouse in his ...
 3 Said the waiter, 'Don't ...
 4 And wave it ...
 5 Or the rest will be wanting one ...!'

 6 A glutton who came from the ... ,
 7 When asked at what hour he would ... ,
 8 Replied, 'At ... ,
 9 At three, five and ... ,
10 And eight and a quarter past ...'.

11 There was an old lady of ...
12 Whose nose was remarkably ...
13 One day, they ... ,
14 She followed her ... ,
15 For no-one knows which way she ... .

about / bent (= not straight) / chew / Crewe / dine / eleven / grows /
heaven / Kent / nine /-nose / Rhine / sent /-seven / shout / out /
stew (= a dish cooked slowly in water) / suppose / too / wine / went

A3 Correcting tasks

In the following task you will have to correct mistakes in a number of limericks. In
some the lines are jumbled together, in others there is something wrong with the
rhyme scheme or metre.

Task thirty-eight

This time we have mixed three limericks together. Only lines 1 and 3 are in the correct place in each limerick.

There was a young girl in the choir
Used language I dare not pronounce.
Till it reached such a height
Pulled her chair out behind
For careless old people like you!'

A girl who weighed many an ounce
Once dropped her false teeth in the stew.
For a fellow, unkind,
'It's horrid to cater
And they found it next day in the spire.

A certain old lady from Crewe
Whose voice rose up higher and higher
Said a sensitive waiter
It was clear out of sight
Just to see (so he said) if she'd bounce.

Vocabulary notes

to *bounce* is what happens to, for example a rubber ball when you drop it on the floor; to *cater* = either 'look after' or 'provide food for': a *choir* (pronounced kwaɪə) is a group of people who sing together; an *ounce* is a small unit of weight, so 'weighed many an ounce' = 'was very fat'; *sensitive*, here, = 'easily hurt, easily upset'; a *spire* is a thin tower on top of a church; stew was explained in the last task.

Task thirty-nine

In the following limericks the **lines in bold** have the correct rhymes, but something has gone wrong with the others. Suggest correct rhymes for them. (If you find this too difficult, choose the words from the list on the next page.)

1 **A sprightly old man from LA**
2 Once said to his wife, 'If I might,
3 I think I will walk
4 **on my head in the Strand,'**
5 To which she retorted: 'Why not.'

6 **A greedy old grandad from Duns,**
7 Once said he'd eat ninety-nine cakes.
8 At the seventy-ninth,
9 **He unluckily burst,**
10 So the rest were consumed by his boss.

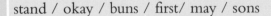

stand / okay / buns / first/ may / sons

Task forty

This time the rhymes are all fine, but something has gone wrong with the **metre**, except in one line per poem, printed in bold. Some words are too long, others too short; or there are too many or too few words.

● See if you can work out what is wrong.

● Then look at the list of words which you will need to use.

● And if that is still too difficult, listen to the tape to hear what needs changing.

> **Vocabulary notes**
> **1st limerick:** *an acquaintance* is someone you know, but not very well; *tame* is the opposite of *wild* (dogs are tame, but lions are usually wild). ·
> **2nd limerick:** a *greedy* person is someone who eats a lot; *gherkins* = pickled cucumbers; to *pickle* = 'to preserve food – vegetables usually – in vinegar or salt water'; *internal workings*, in this poem, means 'the inside of her body'.
> **3rd limerick:** a *blaze* is a strongly burning fire; *charred* means 'burned black on the outside'; to *glow* = 'to burn gently, but brightly'.

awfully / could not / fear / friends / fuel / her / heightened / man / remind / young

There was an old gentleman of Khartoum
Who kept two tame sheep in his room.
To make him think, he said
Of two acquaintances of his who were dead;
But he was completely unable to remember of whom.

A greedy lady called Perkins
Was fond of small gherkins.
She devoured forty-three
One day for tea
And pickled all of her internal workings.

When the shortage of things to burn made it hard,
To maintain the big blaze in our yard;
We decided to throw on Aunt Flo,
Who began to glow,
But I regret to say that she became somewhat charred.

Here is a well-known limerick which breaks the rules of both rhyme and metre. Why it does so should be obvious.

Two poets from Lytham,
had simply no sense of rhythm.
Their limericks would rhyme
only occasionally
So the editor sadly rejected all their work
And off they went taking their poems with 'em.

A4 Limericks demonstrating aspects of fast speech

a) weak forms of grammatical items

The last poem contained the rhymes *Lytham / rhythm / with 'em*. The last is only a rhyme if you use the weakest form of the pronoun *them*. The following poems all use weak forms of pronouns or of other grammatical items dealt with earlier in the book.

The most common pronoun used this way is the weakest form of *them*, pronounced əm.This is because it provides a rhyme for place names ending in <-ham> which, as you may remember from Part 1, is also pronounced əm.

> **Vocabulary notes**
> *brand-new* = 'completely new'; *knickers* are women's underpants; a *quid* = 'a pound'; a *thrifty* person is very careful with money; a *vicar* is a minister of religion.

Said a man to his wife down in Sydenham,
'My trousers – now where have you hidden 'em ? (= them)
It's perfectly true
That they're far from brand–new
But I foolishly left half a quid in 'em!'

A thrifty young fellow of Shoreham
Made brown paper trousers and wore 'em;
He looked nice and neat
Till he bent in the street
To pick up a pin; then he tore 'em.

There was a young lady of Twickenham
whose shoes were too tight to walk quick in 'em.
She came back from a walk
looking whiter than chalk
and took 'em both off and was sick in 'em.

There was a young lady of Tottenham
who'd no manners, or else she'd forgotten 'em.
At tea at the vicar's
she tore off her knickers
because, she explained, she felt hot in 'em.

And remember that <-ster> at the end of place names also contains schwa, which means it can rhyme with the weakest form of the pronoun *her*.

> There was a young lady from Gloucester
> Whose parents thought that they had lost 'er (= her)
> From the fridge came a sound
> And at last she was found;
> The trouble was how to defrost 'er.

The possessive adjective *her* also weakens to schwa in its shortest form.

> There was a young lady of Ryde
> who ate some green apples and died.
> The apples fermented   (= became alcohol)
> inside the lamented,   (= the dead person)
> and made cider inside 'er inside.   (= inside her inside)
>   = əm meid saɪdər ɪn 'saɪdər ɪn 'saɪd

Finally, here's a rhyme which only works if two sounds are elided.

> There was a young fellow named Sydney
> who drank till he ruined his kidney.
> It shrivelled and shrank
> as he sat there and drank.
> But he had a good time at it, didn'(t) (h)e?

b) To end the section on limericks, here is something I wrote just to demonstrate that it is possible to produce a poem, each stanza of which is a limerick.

So you think you've got problems!

> There's really no problem with lexis,
> it's easy whatever your sex is.
> The words are the same
> from sleepy old Thame
> right over to Galveston, Texas.
>
> And syntax should cause you no pain,
> there's no need for worry or strain.
> They use the same pattern
> from Leeds to Manhattan,
> from southern New Zealand to Maine.
>
> But 'pron' is a different matter;
> the brightest of brains it can shatter.
> You start off confused,
> aggrieved and bemused,
> and end up as mad as a hatter.

A student of mine from Algiers
would frequently burst into tears,
for her rhythm and stress
were a terrible mess
and yet she'd been studying for years.

Another from Lima (Peru)
said 'Teacher, just what should I do ?
Does 'cough' rhyme with 'rough'
and 'bough' with 'enough'',
and what about 'thorough' and 'through' ?'

Another young student from Spain
said 'Teacher, please could you explain
why 'bury' and 'ban'
and 'very' and 'van'
are different ? To me they're the same !!'

'That's easy', said Tanaka-san,
(a nice, unassuming young man)
'but 'red', 'right' and 'wrong'
and 'led', 'light' and 'long'
are problems to us from Japan.'

An obstinate student from Spa
refused to acknowledge the schwa.
He said 'go to town'
and 'jump up and down'.
That's taking things rather too far !

So students and teachers all sigh,
they jibber and shiver and cry,
tearing hair from their heads,
sobbing late in their beds,
they wonder if succour is nigh.

But don't worry, help is in sight.
I'm really aware of your plight.
Just taking a look
at my latest book
will help you (at least it just might).

B Other types of poem

B1 'My father's job's more important than yours' by Alan Maley

This is the first of two ingenious poems in this section by Alan Maley (see the page opposite). In this one , which is in rhyming couplets, there is only one rhyme, /ɔːz/; in other words, the second line always ends with a word which rhymes with *yours*.

Task forty-one

Choose the missing word at the end of each couplet. (Note that I have mixed in a few words which do not belong there, and that one word appears twice in the poem!)

cause	jaws	stores	shores	laws
claws	roars	wars	caws	applause
doors (× 2)	boars	pause	bores	stores

Task forty-two

Now choose an adjective which describes each different job. The word must do two different things:

a) It must fit the **meaning**. Thus a doctor's job can be called *useful*, but you wouldn't say *dangerous*, for example.

b) It must also fit the *metre* (the *rhythm*, in other words). If you look at the first lines of each couplet you will see that there are three types of adjective:

● one syllable with <-er> added to make it comparative

● two syllables with front stress. i.e. ■ ○;

● three syllables with stress on the middle syllable. i.e. ○ ■ ○.

In fact, before you look for an adjective, read out the line with the missing adjective replaced by DAH du (= ■ ○) or du DAH du (= ○ ■ ○).

ONE	2	3	ONE	2	3	ONE	2	3	ONE
1 My father's **job**		is	much DAH	duh	than	**yours**:			
2 My father's **job**		is	more DAH	duh	than	**yours**:			
3 My father's **job**'s	more	duh	DAH	duh	than	**yours**:			

So think about the **metre** as well as the **meaning** when you choose the adjectives. Again there are a number of extra adjectives. And sometimes more than one adjective will fit.

daring	tiring	demanding	healthy	brave
odder	important	stranger	skilled	unusual
amazing	dangerous	exhausting	longer	useful

My father's job is more (1) .... than yours:
He's a doctor who works day and night without (2) ....

My father's job is more (3) .... than yours:
He's a stuntman who jumps out of aeroplane (4) ....

My father's job's more (5) .... than yours:
He's a High Court Judge who helps make the (6) ....

My father's job's more (7) .... than yours:
He's the TV technician who records the (8) ....

My father's job is much (9) .... than yours:
He tames lions and tigers and cuts off their (10) ....

My father's job is more (11) .... than yours:
He's a farmer who spends all his time out of (12) ....

Now, if only your father was as useful as mine:
Then everything here would be perfectly fine!

B2 'Light and shadows' by Alan Maley

Task forty-three

This poem is also in rhyming couplets. Within every line there are two words or phrases which are opposite in meaning. Sometimes they are true opposites, as in *saint / sinner* or *loser / winner*; more often the choice of word is less clear. I have cut out two words in each verse, one rhyming word at the end of a line, the other inside a line. (The final couplet has both rhyming words missing.) Start by finding the rhymes, then look for the words which will complete the opposite meaning.

beast	doubt	famine	free	health	life
listener	most	peace	poverty	pride	priest
rule	side	silence	thief	wise	worry

Vocabulary notes
a *chatterbox* is a person who can't stop talking;
a *famine* is when there is very little food and people begin to die of hunger;
strife is a rare, slightly poetic word meaning 'battle, fighting'.

Inside every saint there's a sinner.
Inside every loser there's a winner.

Inside every (1) .... there's a feast.
Inside every lover there's a (2) ....

Inside every (3) .... man there's a fool.
Inside every chaos there's a (4) ....

Inside every certainty there's (5) ....
Inside every (6) .... there's a shout.

Inside every death there is (7) ....
Inside every (8) .... there is strife.

Inside every good man there's a (9) ....
Inside every (10) .... there's relief.

Inside every (11) .... man there's a prisoner.
Inside every chatterbox there's a (12) ....

Inside every general there's a (13) ....
Inside every (14) .... there's a least.

Inside some (15) .... is wealth
Inside some sickness there is (16) ....

Inside humble acts there is (17) ....
Inside everything we find its other (18) ....

B3 'Going shopping'

Start off by listening to the poem without looking at the text. It has a rather more complicated rhyming scheme than the last two: A A B C C B. In other words you have: a rhyming couplet followed by an non-rhyming third line, then a second rhyming couplet followed by a line which rhymes with the third. The metre is different as well. The scheme carries over six lines and goes like this:

		ONE	TWO	(THREE)
A	Every	time she goes out	shopping	
A	Mary	Williams drives a	whopping	
B	great big	lorry just to	carry all she	buys (pause, pause)
C	For her	family's so	large	
C	that she	really needs a	barge	
B	(there are	twenty-four of	ev(e)ry shape and size).	

So there are two main beats in the A and C lines, with three in the B lines. Pay close attention to the beat or you will try to fit in words which match the meaning but not the metre.

And when you read the poem aloud, remember what you have learned from earlier in the book. The unstressed grammatical words *and* and *of* must be very short or you will not keep to the beat. So careful with *bread an(d) jam an(d) honey*; *jump an(d) cheer an(d) shout* and *a sack of macaroni*, for example.

But please don't read it like a machine. Think of the meaning. Listen to the way the voice goes up and down. And don't think that the end of a line always means the end of a grammatical unit. Sometimes it does as in:

Every time she goes out shopping.

But not in:

Mary Williams drives a whopping.

Mary Williams doesn't drive a *'whopping'*; she drives a *whopping great big lorry* (= a very big lorry). You should read lines 1 to 3 like this:

Every time she goes out shopping

Mary Williams drives a whopping great big lorry just to carry all she buys.

Vocabulary notes

a *barge* is a long, flat boat for carrying goods on a river or canal; *boloney* is a type of sausage (originally from *Bologna*, in Italy); *mutton* is meat from sheep; *tradesmen* are people who own shops (*tradespeople* wouldn't fit the metre); *whopping big* means *extremely big*.

Task forty-four

Choose from the following words the ones to fit gaps 1 to 10 in the poem. Only one will be possible at the end of lines, but there may be more than one possibility inside a line. Try out the DAH du du system to see if a word fits the metre as well as the meaning.

age / all / bag / big / bit / bus / can / car / cash / cat / city / clap / confetti / dog / down / each / every / gets / hat / height / jump / money / packet / pound / sack / shout / spaghetti / tin / town / truck / up / village / wave

Task forty-five

Now fill gaps 11 to 22. This time see how quickly you can spot the possibilities. There are three words for each gap. Sometimes only one fits, sometimes two, sometimes all three.

who	jeans	Charley	must	sugar	time
they	beans	Peter	can	chocolate	cash
he	means	Sally	does	biscuits	money
bread	meeting	wheat	kilo	yoghurt	crates
cake	heating	meat	pound	cream	pounds
coke	baking	meet	tin	cheese	bags

Every time she goes out shopping
Mary Williams drives a whopping
great big lorry just to carry all she buys.

For her family's so large
that she really needs a barge
(there are twenty-four of every shape and size).

As she drives her lorry (1) ....
to the centre of the (2) ....
all the tradesmen start to (3) .... and cheer and (4) ....

For she spends vast sums of (5) ....
just on bread and jam and honey
(not to mention all the wine and beer and stout).

And (6) .... day she buys (7) ....
(that's for Margaret, Fred and Betty)
and some mutton chops with very little fat.

And a metre of baloney
with a (8) .... of macaroni
and a (9) .... of something tasty for the (10) ....

Then there's artichokes and (11) ....
and a case of tinned sardines,
with some anchovies and cabbages and steak.

And especially for (12) ....
(as he likes things slightly sweeter)
lots of (13) .... and a slice or two of (14) ....

She buys mustard by the (15) .... ,
salt and pepper (freshly ground)
and vast quantities of butter, milk and (16) .... ,

And for Cathy, Joe and Reg
((17) .... eat nothing else but veg)
several (18) .... of carrots, radishes and peas.

As for her, what (19) .... she eat,
is it fish or fruit or (20) .... ?
What's the kind of thing that mothers like the best ?

Well she's got no (21) .... for eating
for she's cooking or she's (22) ....
up the food she's bought to serve to all the rest.

B4 'Song for London'

This poem/song, with its simple **ABCB** rhyming scheme, sums up the way I feel about London. Yes, it's noisy, polluted, dirty and sometimes dangerous; but it's also one of the most exciting cities in the world, with lively street markets, greenery and water and just about the best theatre, art and music scenes you will find anywhere.

You can work on this poem in different ways:

1 Just read it and try to guess what the missing words are. (Usually just one word is missing, but gaps 4, 19, 22, 29 and 35 contain three words each.)

2 Look at the words on page 106 and choose the ones which fit.

3 Use it as a dictation, by listening to the poem and filling the gaps.

But take care if you try methods **1** or **2**. Some words may fit the **meaning** but not the **metre**. So say a line out loud, with a du DAH or a DAH duh duh, and so on, to replace the missing word. Think. Is there one syllable missing here? Two? Three? Then try out the word you think fits.

Pre-task and vocabulary notes
Brick Lane and *Camden Town* have lively markets at the weekend;
Dr Samuel Johnson was an 18th century writer, best known for his dictionary;
to *choke* usually = 'not to be able to breathe';
to *glint* = 'to shine when the light catches an object, a ring, for example';
to *hurtle* = 'to move very fast, usually past something else';
to *lurk* = 'to hide in wait for someone, perhaps to attack them';
to *mess up* = 'to make something dirty or untidy';
potholes are very big holes, especially dangerous for cyclists like me;
a *spyhole* is a little glass-covered hole in a door, so you can see who a visitor is but they can't see you;
trash = *rubbish*: 'things thrown away'.

Task forty-six

Choose the missing single words from the following list. Sometimes more than one can fit a gap.

Part A

glad	rising	weather	tubes	fog	at
arrows	shining	explain	for	rainbows	smog
pleased	dirt	by	happy	agree	fumes
buses	trains	diamonds	setting	gold	

Part B

in	use	speak	die	film	scared
darkness	know	drive	play	after	lorries
cry	buses	concert	afraid	midnight	dark
pub	cycle	nightfall	for	look	cars
frightened					

Part C

cats	walk	traffic	decide	put	trash
helicopters	dogs	night	agree	but	rubbish
up	take	down	sleeping	stroll	though
cycle	pollution	dark	breathing	get	

Task forty-seven

Now sort out the following words to fill gaps 4, 19, 22, 29 and 35.

at	at	of	to	why	the
you	care	leave	tell	seems	eight
tired	door	life			

A   The roads are full of potholes
and the streets are full of trash,
the pavements lined with youngsters
asking, 'can you spare some cash?'

The (1) .... are packed to bursting
and the (2) .... always late.
If you want to get to town (3) .... noon
you'd better (4) _____ .

But when the sun is (5) ....
and the river glints like (6) .... ,
and the bridges curve like (7) .... ,
then the city takes its hold.

and I'm **(8)** .... to be in London,
though I really can't **(9)** ....
And London's where I live
despite the **(10)** .... , the **(11)** .... and rain.

B   The **(12)** .... hurtle past me
as I **(13)** .... to my work.
If I come home after **(14)** ....
I'm **(15)** .... of who might lurk.

You hardly **(16)** .... your neighbours
(17) .... 20 years or more,
and **(18)** .... a little spyhole
when someone's **(19)** _____ .

But when I'm sitting waiting
for the **(20)** .... to begin,
or a **(21)** .... by some young writer
makes me think that we might win,

then I'm glad to be in London,
though it's hard to **(22)** _____ .
And London is the city
where I'll live until I **(23)** ....

C   The **(24)** .... mess up the pavement,
The kids daren't use the park;
The traffic wrecks the daytime;
alarms disturb the **(25)** ....

The **(26)** .... chokes the gutters,
(27) .... fills the air,
old folks have trouble **(28)** ....
and no-one **(29)** _____ .

But when I **(30)** .... at weekends
through Brick Lane or Camden Town,
I realise that, though
there's plenty here to **(31)** .... me **(32)** ....

I **(33)** .... with Doctor Johnson
(**(34)** .... I can't speak for my wife)
that a man who's tired of London
is a man who's **(35)** _____ .

'Failure'

Vocabulary notes

when the stock market *crashes* the value of shares goes down;

a *fake* is something (usually a work of art) which is not by the artist expected;

a *pheasant* is a game bird, i.e. a bird bred for shooting and eating;

to *pot* – 'to hit a ball into the pocket' when playing billiards or snooker. If you aim for one colour and hit another you lose points;

to be given the *sack* is to be fired, to lose your job;

tame is the opposite of *wild*;

a *wren* is a small song-bird.

Task forty-eight

This is another poem in rhyming couplets. As you can see from the first couplet it is about a man for whom everything goes wrong. And something has gone wrong with the poem, too. Your task is to match the endings to the beginnings of each line.

1 He studied so hard but the others all passed.
He tried to be first but he always came last.

2 He learned Japanese
He lost his umbrella

a) but the weather decided to break.
b) which proved to be tame.

3 He wore his best suit
He trained as an actor

c) who couldn't stand men.
d) the day of the rain.

4 He aimed for the yellow
He worked very hard

e) but landed a shark.
f) but nobody came.

5 He invested in shares
He collected fine china

g) while the others wore jeans.
h) but wounded a wren.

6 He bought a Picasso
He stripped

i) which just wouldn't bark.
j) but nobody went.

7 He held a big party
He hunted a tiger

k) but was transferred to Spain
l) until, sadly, he died.

8 He bought a huge watchdog
He fished for a salmon

m) but all of it smashed.
n) while the others all lied.

9 He played at roulette
He opened a cafe

o) but was given the sack.
p) which turned out a fake.

10 He shot at a pheasant
He married a woman

q) but potted the black.
r) but he lost every cent.

11 He stuck to the truth
And so it went on

s) then joined the marines.
t) then the stock market crashed.

B6 'Mustn't grumble'

We British are known for our understatements. If you ask people from the USA how they are, they're likely to reply 'Fine!' , 'Great!' or 'Never been better!', all with firm falling tones. In Britain you're more likely to hear 'Not too bad', or 'Could be worse', with that very British fall-rise. My two favourite replies are 'mustn't grumble' and 'can't complain'. And it was while thinking about how these normally involve both elision and assimilation – ˈmʌsəŋ ˈgrʌmbl̩, ˈkɑːŋ kəmˈpleɪn – that the idea for this poem came to me.

Task forty-nine

Here are the missing words from the poem (with a few extra thrown in). As you can see, they all rhyme either with *grumble* or *complain*. Fill each gap with an appropriate word. You may use an English dictionary if you wish.

train	brain	stain	cane	grain	again
rain	lane	main	explain	chain	insane
rumble	tumble	humble	fumble	bumble	stumble
crumble (see **d**) below)			jumble (see **e**) below)		

Vocabulary notes

a) a *cockroach* is a dark-brown or black insect, sometimes found in kitchens;

b) the 'naughty snowflakes' refer to one winter when trains in the south of England stopped running because, as British Rail explained, the snow was 'the wrong kind';

c) BSE – *bovine spongiform encephalopathy* – (popularly known as 'mad cow disease') has already spread from sheep to cows, and some people fear it may spread to humans as well;

d) a *crumble* is a type of pudding, with a topping made of flour (or flour and muesli) mixed with brown sugar;

e) *jumble* is used in the sense of *jumble sale*, where people give away things (especially clothes) to be sold for charity.

'Mustn't grumble', 'Can't complain':
our traditional refrain.
Don't be pushy, best be humble.
Don't complain, and never grumble.

Broken pavings make you (1) .... ?
Cockroach in your apple (2) .... ?
Mustn't grumble, can't complain.

8.05 is late (3) .... ?
Naughty snowflakes stopped the (4) .... ?
Don't complain, you shouldn't grumble.

Government begins to (5) .... ?
Housing prices start to (6) .... ?
Mustn't grumble, can't complain.

Trees are killed by acid (7) .... ?
BSE attacks the (8) .... ?
Don't complain, no need to grumble.

Kiddy's clothes come from the (9) .... ?
Balkan guns begin to (10) .... ?
Do not ask them to (11) .... ;
just accept it, don't complain.
Mustn't grumble,
Mustn't grumble,
Mustn't grumble.

B7 'When the cat's away, the mice will play'

This is a poem in which every rhyming word ends in <-ed>, in other words is a past participle, either used as a verb or an adjective.

Task fifty

Many of the verbs are rather formal. So your first task, before you look at the poem, is to match some of the formal words with their less formal equivalents.

1 augmented		a) full of (something you don't want)
2 congested		b) begged (someone to do something)
3 transpired		c) disagreed
4 aggravated		d) over-crowded, usually with traffic or people
5 satiated		e) went away (like rain drops in the sun)
6 dissented		f) increased, made bigger
7 evaporated		g) full-up, perhaps over full
8 conceded		h) annoyed, fed-up
9 pleaded		i) admitted that someone else was right
10 infested		j) happened

Task fifty-one

Here are some less formal verbs, the meanings of which may be confused. Match the verbs, their definitions, and the things that they collocate with (i.e. are usually found with).

verbs

shattered / tattered / slashed / gashed

definitions

cut very deeply	broken into very small pieces
old and torn	cut with long violent strokes

collocations

skin, wood etc.	glass, crockery etc.
clothing, flags etc.	people, vegetation, prices etc.

Task fifty-two

Now look at the poem on page 112. The rhyme scheme, as you can see, goes ABBA BCCB CDDC, and so on. Note also that the A and E rhymes are re-used later in the poem.

The missing words are all jumbled together below. Your task is to write each word where it belongs according to rhyme. (Note that *rested* and *waited* are used twice.)

aggravated / augmented / blunted / conceded / confessed / congested / contented / created / depressed / dissented / evaporated / exaggerated / excited / gashed / hated / hired / impressed / infested / inspired / invited / needed / pleaded / posted / rested (×2) / satiated / scattered / shattered / slashed / stated / tattered / tested / transpired / trashed / united / waited (×2)

A suggested / ....

....

B desired / ....

C unimpeded / ....

D delighted / ....

E elated / ....

....

F be-spattered / ....

G smashed / ....

H possessed / ....

I relented / ....

J boasted / ....

K wanted / ....

Note: the final rhyme (*wanted*/*blunted*) is controversial. My feeling is that *want* is increasingly pronounced to rhyme with *hunt*, *blunt* etc. This is certainly the way I pronounce it, and I think I'm far from alone.

Task fifty-three

Check the key for Task 51, on page 169, to make sure that you have grouped the rhyming words together. Your final task, using the dictionary where necessary, is to see which type of rhyme is needed, then fit the words into place. All the verbs should be in the dictionary with the possible exception of *trash*, which means 'to ruin, to wreck' (i.e. to make something only fit to be thrown away as trash).

A In the Spring my wife suggested
B what she'd secretly desired;
B I agreed it was **(1)** ....
A and we'd come back really **(2)** ....

B So it finally **(3)** ....
C that we went off unimpeded,
C kids the last thing that we **(4)** .... ,
B in the caravan we'd **(5)** ....

C So they cried and wept and **(6)** .... ?
D Course they didn't; all delighted
D they accepted, quite **(7)** ....
C 'Good for you', the lads **(8)** ....

D 'Off you go!' they said, **(9)** .... ;
E so we drove off, quite elated,
E while they phoned (they might have **(10)** .... !)
D to the various friends **(11)** ....

E Three weeks later, **(12)** .... ,
A we returned, completely **(13)** .... ,
A but our patience soon was **(14)** ....
E and our joy **(15)** ....

A For the house was mouse-**(16)** .... ,
F rooms uncleaned, the walls be-spattered,
F sinks unwashed and dishes **(17)** .... ,
A everywhere with kids **(18)** ....

F Curtains all completely **(19)** .... ;
G telly, CD, video smashed;
G all my records warped and **(20)** .... ;
F glasses, windows, all were **(21)** ....

G Sunday clothes were ripped and (22) ....

H by some fool no doubt possessed

H (or else clinically (23) ....);

G all the house completely (24) .... !

H Deeply shamed the boys (25) ....

E they'd indeed (26) ....;

E loathed the chaos they'd (27) ....

H We, however, quite (28) ....

E by their demeanour simply (29) ....

I that we had indeed relented.

I Fact is, secretly (30) .... ,

E we were far from (31) ....

I and were pleased, our joy (32) ....

E by the thought that we both (33) ....

E all our things, indeed had (34) ....

I to replace them. None (35) .... ,

J all agreed, in fact we boasted

K of the marvellous things we wanted;

K but our happiness was (36) .... (see note on page 112):

J uninsured – the cheque not (37) ....

Part 5

SOUNDS AND MOVEMENT

Poems are included in this part if:

- they contain examples of **onomatopoeia**, that is to say, words such as *whisper*, *bang* and *hiss* which imitate **sounds,** or

- the metre is based on a **rhythm** to be found in the real world, that of a train or a horse , for example. And finally,

- they deal with some means of transport.

(Of course, some poems may combine two or all of the above.)

Most are included simply to provide further practice in listening and in reading aloud while keeping to a solid beat. But the first two offer you a chance to see if you can match onomatopoeic nouns and verbs to the things in the world to which they refer.

Both are written in rhyming couplets (AA BB CC, remember) and provide a catalogue of sounds; but 'Noise' is a celebration while 'Mornings' is a complaint.

Task fifty-four

Listen to each poem once or twice, without reading it, just to get the feel of the rhythm. Read each poem as many times as you like, **without listening to it any more,** and try to match the onomatopeic words to their referents. If you find this too difficult, listen to the poems two or three times more, then try to fill the gaps again.

Note that in 'Noise' the onomatopoeic words have been cut out and jumbled together, whereas in 'Mornings' it is the referents which are missing.

Vocabulary notes
crowing is the sound made by a cockeral; *galvanised* = 'made of metal'; a *gamut* = 'a wide range'; a *hoof* = 'the foot of a horse'; to *numb* = 'to make something feel dead or insensitive'; a *pail* = 'a bucket, a metal object for carrying water'; a *rifle* = 'a type of gun'; *tattoo* (here) = 'a continuous drumming sound'

'Noise' by Jessie Pope

I like noise.
The **(1)** .... of the boy, the **(2)** .... of a hoof,
the **(3)** .... of rain on a galvanised roof.
the **(4)** .... of traffic, the **(5)** .... of a train,
the **(6)** .... of machinery numbing the brain,
the switching of wires in an overhead tram,
the **(7)** .... of the wind, a door on the **(8)** .... ,
the **(9)** .... of the thunder, the **(10)** .... of the waves,
the din of a river that races and raves,
the **(11)** .... of a rifle, the **(12)** .... of a pail,
the strident tattoo of a swift- **(13)** ....–ping sail.
From any old sound that the silence destroys
arises a gamut of soul–stirring joys.
I like noise.

boom / clank / crack / crash / hubbub / rattle / roar / rush / slam / slap / throb / thud / whoop

---

Note: all of these words (except hubbub) can function either as noun or as verb

'Mornings' by Alan Maley

The previous poem showed how sounds can be enjoyable and exciting; this one is written from the opposite point of view. In this case the onomatopoeic words are all given and you have to put their referents into the gaps. (It may help you to know that as the poem goes on the noises get louder and **louder** and **louder**).

Vocabulary notes:
birds *chirp* and cockerels *crow*; to *stifle* is to cut off a sound, as if a hand is placed over your mouth

Rustling (1) ....
Shuffling (2) ....
Creaking (3) ....
Stifled groans,
Chirping, crowing,
Noses blowing,
(4) .... flushing,
(5) .... gushing,
(6) .... clatter,
(7) .... chatter,
Neighbours singing,
(8) .... ringing,
Radios tuning,
(9) .... booming,
(10) .... thrumming,
(11) .... drumming,
(12) .... thunder –
I just wonder
at the NOISE!

Bath taps / bones / Breakfast / Coffee cups / feet / Jet planes / Motor bikes / Power drills / sheet / Telephones / Toilets / Traffic

Windy nights by Rodney Bennett

This is a bit of a tongue-twister, especially if you have problems with <r> sounds.

> Rumbling in the chimneys,
> Rattling at the doors,
> Round the roofs and round the roads
> The rude wind roars,
> Raging through the darkness,
> Racing through the trees,
> Racing off again across
> The great grey seas.

Rush hour by Maisie Cobby

Here are two which give good practise in <s> and <sh> sounds.

> What a rush,
> What a crush,
> What a fuss, fuss, fuss!
> Everybody's running for the five o'clock bus.

Look out by Paul Edmonds

> Look out, look out a motor is coming!
> Look out, look out a motor is coming!
> Here it comes splashing
> And hooting and dashing
> Look out, look out, look out!

Our big steeple clock by Ian Dunlop

This poem starts off really slow. You must imagine a big clock on top of a church steeple, ticking away slowly. The kitchen clock is faster, while the wrist watch is fastest of all.

1 Our big steeple clock
   Goes tick-tock
   Tick-tock

2 Our new kitchen clock
   Goes tick-tack, tick-tack
   tick-tack, tick-tack.

3 Our little wrist watch
   Goes ticker-tacker, ticker-tacker
   ticker-tacker, tick.

Three seasons by Ian Dunlop

More practise in consonants sounds here:

- the /w/ of *white, walls, windows, wind, what wonderful weather.*

- the /s/ of *snow, sun, pass*

- the /z/ at the end of *walls, windows, nose, toes, showers, flowers, breeze, bees, raspberries, strawberries* as well as in *buzzing*.

This poem contains a lot of long vowels, so make sure you prolong words such as *walls, snow, nose, toes* and *breeze*. And make sure these long vowels contrast with the short words.

So *look at the snow* and *what shall I wear* both go DAH du du DAH; that is, they have the ■ ○ ○ ■ pattern. And *the breeze in the trees* is ○ ■ ○ ○ ■.

Winter
White walls and windows
Look at the snow, look at the snow.
Cold nose and cold toes,
Look at the snow, look at the snow.

Spring
Wind and rain and sun and showers.
What shall I wear? What shall I wear?
A plastic mack or a hat with flowers?
What shall I wear? What shall I wear?

Summer
The breeze in the trees and the buzzing of the bees,
What wonderful weather, what wonderful weather.
Raspberries and strawberries and 'Pass the cream, please',
What wonderful weather, what wonderful weather.

The engine driver by Clive Sansom

Now we move on to poems where the metre imitates the rhythm of a train; at least, that of an old-fashioned steam train. Don't look up *jickety-can* in the dictionary; it is an invented piece of onomatopoeia.

The train goes running along the line,
Jickety-can, jickety-can,
I wish it was mine, I wish it was mine
Jickety-can, jickety-can,
The engine driver stands in front –
He makes it run, he makes it shunt

Out of the town,
Out of the town,
Over the hill,
Over the down,
Under the bridges
Across the lea,
Over the ridges
And down to the sea.

With a jickety-can, jickety-can,
Jickety-can, jickety-can,
Jickety-can, jickety-can ...

Slinky Hank the railway rat by David Orme

David Orme takes the same train rhythm to show the speed at which Slinky Hank, a 'railway rat', works as he 'nips' around (= gets around quickly) so fast that you don't notice him.

Vocabulary notes
to *slink* means 'to move along quietly so nobody can see you'; to *nibble* is the way rats and mice eat; *slimy* means 'covered in wet, sticky dirt'; *domain* means 'kingdom'; if your smell is *rank* then you probably haven't washed for weeks; *clinker* is burnt-out coal.

Slinky Hank! Slinky Hank,
He lurks by the tracks where it's cold and dank
He nibbles at feasts in a rusty tank!
When he sees the lights of the midnight train,
Hank'll creep out from his slimy domain
And mutter 'disgraceful! it's late again!
They'd do better these days on a coach or a plane'
Yes, it's Slinky Hank, Slinky Hank,
He hoards his treasures like cash in a bank
In a hole in a culvert that's smelly and rank,
A bag, a bottle, a bone or two,
A sole with a hole from a signalman's shoe
Your junk's a dinner for Slinky Hank!
Slinky Hank! Slinky Hank!
He's a rat with a mission, a rat of high rank,
He cleans up the railway so we can all thank
The prince of the clinker,
Slinky Hank!

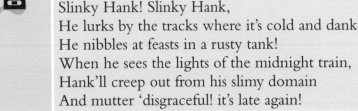

From a railway carriage by Robert Louis Stevenson

This is a famous poem from Stevenson's 'A Child's Garden of Verses'.
It contains a large number of words the spelling of which is predictable from the pronunciation: notably, *bridges, hedges, witches, ditches, battle, cattle, clamber, scramble, bramble, gather, glimpse,* and so on. Just think about how they sound and how they are spelled, **then** worry about the meaning.

Faster than fairies, faster than witches,
Bridges and houses, hedges and ditches;
And charging along like troops in a battle,
All through the meadows the horses and cattle:
All of the sights of the hill and the plain
Fly as thick as driving rain;
And ever again, in the wink of an eye,
Painted stations whistle by.
Here is a child who clambers and scrambles,
All by himself and gathering brambles;
Here is a cart run away in the road
Lumping along with man and load;
And here is a mill, and there is a river:
Each a glimpse and gone for ever.

Victoria by Eleanor Farjeon

In this poem, Eleanor Farjeon expresses her joy when she is able to leave London to head down to the Sussex coast. Sadly, many of these villages no longer have railway stations.

From Victoria I can go
To Pevensey Level and Piddinghoe,
Open Winkins and Didling Hill,
Three Cups Corner and Selsey Bill.
I'm the happiest one in all the nation
When my train runs out of Victoria Station.
But O the day when I come to town
From Ditchling Beacon and Duncton Down,
Bramber Castle and Wisborough Green,
Cissbury Ring and Ovingdean!
I'm the sorriest one in all the nation
When my train runs into Victoria Station.

My mother said

This is an old anonymous poem (that means, we don't know who wrote it). As it gets near the end, and the speaker jumps on the horse, the number of unstressed syllables increases and you have to speak faster to keep to the beat of the horse's hooves.

My mother said, I never should
play with the gypsies in the wood.

If I did then she would say:
'Naughty child to disobey!'

'Your hair shan't curl and your shoes shan't shine,
You gypsy child, you shan't be mine!'

And my father said that if I did,
he'd rap my head with the tea-pot lid.

My mother said that I never should
play with the gypsies in the wood.

The wood was dark, the grass was green;
By came Sally with a tambourine.

I went to sea – no ship to get across;
I paid ten shillings for a blind white horse.

I upped on his back and was off in a crack,
Sally tell my mother I shall never come back.

Windy nights by Robert Louis Stevenson

Here's another poem from Stevenson's 'A Child's Garden of Verses'. It has the rhythm of a galloping horse, that is to say, a horse running as fast as possible.

Whenever the moon and stars are set,
Whenever the wind is high,
All night long in the dark and wet,
A man goes riding by.
Late in the night when the fires are out,
Why does he gallop and gallop about?

Whenever the trees are crying aloud,
And ships are tossed at sea,
By, on the highway, low and loud,
By at the gallop goes he:
By at the gallop he goes, and then
By he comes back at the gallop again.

How they brought the pizzas from Brent to Penge by David Orme

This is an extremely witty parody of Robert Browning's *How they brought the good news from Gent to Aix*. David Orme has kept the galloping rhythm of the original, but the journey is by bicycle, not by horse, the destination is the rather unromantic London suburb of Penge, and what is delivered is not an important message, but some pieces of pizza. (If you teach in London you can get students to trace this epic journey on a good London map.)

The language is a lovely mixture of the archaic (= old-fashioned) and the colloquial.

Archaic sequences include: *we pedalled all three* (l. 2.= 'all three of us pedalled'); *by the boss we'd been told* (l. 11 = 'we'd been told by the boss'); *T'was teatime* (l. 13 = 'it was tea-time'); *paid not a heed* (l. 16 = 'paid no attention, took no notice'); *we pedalled apace* (l. 18 = 'we pedalled fast').

Examples of colloquial language include: *blow this for a lark* (l. 34 = 'I've had enough, that's my lot!'; *Matey* (l. 34 = a form of 'Mate', a friendly term of address); *I'm whacked* (l. 34 = 'I'm tired out'); *where the heck* (l. 42 = a softer version of 'where the hell..!); *he walloped my bike* (l. 46 = 'he banged my bike').

Note that some words have been put in **bold**. These need special stressing if you want to keep to the beat.

1   I sprang to the saddle, and Doris, and he,
2   I pedalled, Dick pedalled, we pedalled all three,
3   'Beep beep' went my watch as we swerved down the street
4   'Beep' echoed a car that we'd missed by two feet,
5   Behind shut the door, the sun sank in the west
6   And down Edgware Road we three pedalled abreast.

7   We'd no time for talking, we pedalled like mad
8   With Dick out ahead (he's a healthy young lad)
9   We weaved through the traffic, took our life in our hands
10 By quick overtaking on the blind side of vans.
11 We all had to speed it, by the boss we'd been told
12 That no-one likes pizzas all crusty and cold.

13 T'was teatime at starting, now while we went past
14 Hyde Park Corner poor Doris cried out 'not so fast!
15 My saddle's all wobbly, I think it's worked loose'.
16 But Dick paid not a heed to this feeble excuse.
17 We went faster than ever down Grosvenor Place,
18 Past Victoria Station we pedalled apace.

19 Then out stepped a policeman in Vauxhall Bridge Road,
20 So we flattened his toes with the weight of our load;
21 The lights on the river flashed clear as we passed
22 And at Kennington Oval we slowed down at last.
23 'What's the best way from here?' our leader, Dick, said.
24 So I looked up the route in my old A to Z.

25 So all went quite well till at Camberwell Green
26 Dick clashed with a cabby all sour-faced and mean;
27 His bike fell to the road with a terrible sound
28 And ham and salami spread over the ground;
29 Onions and anchovies, all gone to waste;
30 The cabby just smirked and said 'more speed, less taste'.

31 So **we** were left pedalling, Doris and I,
32 We puffed **up** Denmark Hill with a groan and a sigh;
33 But the strain was too much, at the top Doris cracked;
34 'Blow this for a lark,' she said, 'Matey, I'm whacked!'
35 She got off her bike, she sat down in the street
36 And inspected the blisters that throbbed on her feet.

37 So Doris went home, though I threatened revenge,
38 Now I had to deliver the pizzas to Penge;
39 I hurtled through Dulwich, past Forest Hill station,
40 saw Penge in the distance through tears of elation;
41 The house on the left, with the door painted green;
42 I banged, 'So you've come! where the heck have you been!

43 You were so long in coming,' the customer said,
44 'we cooked up a meal from the freezer instead.
45 So eat your own pizza!' he said with a roar
46 And he walloped my bike as he slammed shut the door.
47 So I stood in the road with my front mudguard bent;
48 And that was my thanks for the Pizzas from Brent.

On your bike

I really think I must be the only person in London who regularly rides a bike but can also drive a car. Car and lorry drivers have no idea of the space that cyclists need and are often a great danger to them; and cyclists fail to realise, for example, that motorists do not expect to be overtaken by a cyclist coming up between them and the pavement.

By the way, I do not recommend you to call people *idiots*, *bastards* or *berks* unless you want a fight.

A When I'm on my bike I am the angel of the street;
   I'm courteous and friendly to everyone I meet.

   I never mount the pavement, I just keep to the road;
   I don't infringe in any way the sacred Highway Code.

   I signal to the motorists and make my movements clear;
   I ride along the gutter and I never swerve or veer.

But what about those bastards in their lorries and their cars?
They stare at me suspiciously as if I came from Mars.

That's if they even notice me as zombie-like they drive;
I need my wits about me if I want to stay alive.

They pass and then turn left or open doors right in my face;
I sometimes think that drivers aren't aware we need some space.

So when you see me cycling in my helmet and my mask,
just use a little courtesy; is that too much to ask?

B   Now when I'm at the wheel I'm always perfectly polite;
aware of all the cyclists, sympathetic to their plight.

I follow very carefully the details of the Code;
I flash to let them cut across a really busy road;

I check the nearside mirror just in case there's one in sight;
and take especial care whenever driving late at night.

But what about those bastards cycling merrily along?
You'd think their parents never tried to teach them right from wrong.

They pass you on the left when you are checking to the right,
then wave their stupid fists at you; they do it out of spite.

They go both ways down one-way-streets, turn left when lights are red.
The bloody little idiots deserve to end up dead!

So when you see me in my car while cycling to work,
just use some common sense, can't you, you stupid little berk!

When in my car or on my bike it's very plain to see;
the roads are full of lunatics,
with one exception:
ME!!

A Car called Heapsville by David Orme

Here's another piece by David Orme, this time about an old much-loved car. There are a few words you may not know. There are various names for cars: *bangers* and *heaps* are old, battered cars, while a *limo* (= 'limousine') is a big, expensive car. The following are all parts of a car: the *sill* is at the bottom of the door; the *subframe* is part of the main structure of the car; *upholstery* is what covers the seats; the *wings* are above the front wheels. And the *MOT* (short for 'Ministry of Transport') is the test which every car over three-years old has to pass every year.

She's a **lit**tle red mini
that **rat**tles like a tin.
Her **tyres** are illegal
'cos the **rub**ber's wearing thin.
So don't **brake** too hard
or you'll **send** her in a spin.

The **steer**ing wheel's loose;
there's **rust** in the sill,
but she's a **great** little mover called
.... Heapsville.

When you **drive** away,
you **leave** a heap of dust.
But it **ain't** no dirt,
it's a **pile** of rust.
There's cor**ros**ion in the wings,
and **stretch** in the springs;
there's **moths** in the seat
and **holes** by your feet
so you can **see** the road
passing **by** a treat.

This car's got cool up**ho**lstery.
It's the **on**ly thing that's passed
the M O T.

The **sub**frame creaks
but I **can't** pay the bill,
so I **just** keep on driving that
Heapsville.

She **ne**ver gives up
when you've **got** a full load,
just **drib**bles black oil
all **o**ver the road.

The **door** comes open when you're **turn**ing left
but she's in**sur**ed third party, **fire** and theft.
I **would**n't swap a limo for my **lit**tle red banger
cos she **gets** rock music on an **old** coathanger.

She **blows** out steam
when she **goes** uphill
but I **just** keep on driving that
Heapsville!

The catch by Kit Wright

This one is short and sweet. You should know that the *ignition* is where you put the key to start a car; to *skid* is what happens when a car slips and slides on water or oil; a *spill*, in this sense, is an accident; and *a thousand quid* = a thousand pounds.

You'll receive a
Vauxhall Viva
if you win our
competition.

Oh, well done, Sir,
you have won, Sir,
here's the keys to
the ignition.

Off you go now,
take it slow now,
MIND OUR WALL —
oh dear, a skid, Sir!

What a spill, Sir,
here's our bill, sir:
you owe **us**
a thousand quid, Sir!

Run, then. Run! by Stephen Hirtenstein

This is a chant, with two different voices. Practise this one with a friend, changing the parts round.

A: It's **cold** today,
so I'd **better** put a **coat** on.
It's **freez**ing cold.
I **think** I'll need my **gloves**.

B: Yes, you'd **bet**ter **wrap** up **well**
or you **might** catch a **cold**.

A: The **bus** is coming,
so I'd **bet**ter get a **move** on.

B: Yes, you'd **bet**ter get going
or you'll **have** to get a **cab**.

A: **Here** comes the bus;
I've **real**ly gotta **go**.
I **think** I'm going to **miss** it.

B: Well **run**, then **run**.

127

A: I THINK I'm going to MISS it!

B: Well RUN, then RUN!

A: **Damn!** I've **missed** it.

Tarantella by Hilaire Belloc

This is a beautiful poem, full of the sounds of guitars and the rhythms of Spanish dancing. And Belloc weaves his **rhyming** words (*tedding/spreading/bedding*; *fleas/ tease / Pyrenees*; *glancing/dancing/advancing*; *cheers/jeers*; *tread/dead*; *ground/sound*; *verandah/Miranda*; *twirl/swirl/girl*; *walls/halls/falls* etc.) in with moments of **alliteration** or other recurrences of vowel and consonants sounds (*tedding, tease, tastes of tar*; *ting, tong, tang*; *hammer, hip, hop, hap, hands*; *more, Miranda*; *tread, feet, dead, ground*).

Do you remember an Inn,
Miranda?
Do you remember an Inn?
And the tedding and the spreading
Of the straw for a bedding,
And the fleas that tease in the High Pyrenees?
And the wine that tastes of tar?
And the cheers and the jeers of the young muleteers
(Under the dark of the vine verandah)?
Do you remember an Inn, Miranda,
Do you remember an Inn?
And the cheers and the jeers of the young muleteers
Who hadn't got a penny,
And who weren't paying any,
And the hammer at the doors and the Din?
And the Hip! Hop! Hap!
Of the clap
Of the hands to the twirl and the swirl
Of the girls gone chancing,
Glancing,
Dancing,
Backing and advancing,
Snapping of the clapper to the spin
Out and in —
And the Ting, Tong, Tang of the guitar!
Do you remember an Inn, Miranda,
Do you remember an Inn?

Never more;
Miranda,
Never more.
Only the high peaks hoar:
And Aragon a torrent at the door,
No sound
In the walls of the Halls where falls
The tread
Of the feet of the dead to the ground.
No sound:
Only the boom
Of the far Waterfall like Doom.

Part 6

PART 6

SIMILES, SAYINGS AND SOUNDS

In this final part of the book we will play with the magic of words and rhythm, concentrating on words and phrases which belong so closely together that you have to learn the rhythm of the phrase together with its meaning.

A Similes

If you say that something is *as light as a feather* or *as heavy as lead* you are using a **simile**: comparing one thing with another.

Some similes are so common that they have become **clichés**, expressions you use without thinking about them. Others are more original and cause the listener to think in a new way about what you are referring to.

And some similes are so old that we understand them as a whole, but not the individual words. If, for example, you say that something is *as plain as a pikestaff* we know that it means 'absolutely obvious; 100% clear', but hardly anybody knows what a *pikestaff* actually is. In fact, it was a smooth type of stick, and the simile originally meant 'as smooth as a pikestaff' (i.e. with no lumps, bumps or decorations).

This particular simile, together with several others, is found in the first poem in this section.

As (anonymous)

This is a poem made up entirely of well-known, proverbial, similes. There is heavy stress on the adjectives and nouns, while the grammatical words *and* and *as* are very short, both containing schwa. When you repeat it remember to make the links in, for example, wet‿as‿a / dry‿as‿a / poor‿as‿a / free‿as the‿air.

> **Vocabulary notes**
> *moles* are short-sighted animals which live underground. Their soft skin used to be made into clothes (especially *mole-skin* trousers);
> *partridges* are game birds, i.e. birds bred to be shot and eaten in the autumn. They are *plump* (= 'fat') because they are ready to eat;
> a *pikestaff* (now archaic) was a type of stick with a plain (= smooth) surface;
> Nowadays the expression *as plain as a pikestaff* = 'obvious, self-evident'.

As **wet** as a **fish** – as **dry** as a **bone**;
As **live** as a **bird** – as **dead** as a **stone**;
As **plump** as a **par**tridge – as **poor** as a **rat**;
As **strong** as a **horse** – as **weak** as a **cat**;
As **hard** as **flint** – as **soft** as a **mole**;
As **white** as a **lily** – as **black** as **coal**;
As **plain** as a **pike**staff – as **rough** as a **bear**;
As **tight** as a **drum** – as **free** as the **air**;
As **heavy** as **lead** – as **light** as a **fea**ther;
as **stea**dy as **time** – un**cer**tain as **wea**ther

Sensible similes

Task fifty-five

In this poem, the first line of each couplet is made up of two well-known similes. The second, rhyming, line has been made up by me. I call these 'sensible' similes, since they all make sense (compared to the 'silly similes' which follow).

Your **task** is to put the following adjectives into the correct places in the poem. The first couplet is complete.

Vocabulary notes
common is used here in the sense of 'vulgar, badly educated, badly behaved';
a *fiddle* is a violin (a stringed instrument), though why it should be associated with good health I do not know;
fit in this sense means 'in good condition, in good health';
icing is a sugary topping for cakes, especially for birthdays and Christmas;
keen is used in the sense of 'eager, enthusiastic', though other meanings include 'sharp, acute, strong', as in the expression *a keen sense of smell*;
long locks = 'long hair';
a *peacock* is a male bird, with extremely beautiful tail feathers;
a *rake* is a long garden instrument used to *rake up* (or remove by pulling along the ground) dead leaves, plants etc.;
a *rocker*, in this sense, is a rock musician, especially one who plays loud, older forms of rock music;
a *tether* is a line or rope attaching an animal (horse, goat, dog etc.) to a particular place. When it is *at the end of its tether* it can go no further, so this has come to mean 'frustrated, impatient, ready to crack up'.

tight	proud	steady	cool	thin	poor	sad
bold	keen	strange	fit	strong	blind	happy
wild	clever	deep	common	light	sickly	rough

As white as a lily, as blue as the sky,
as bright as the flags on the Fourth of July.
As (1) .... as a cucumber, (2) .... as a drum,
as (3) .... as a child falling flat on its bum.

As (4) .... as a bat, as (5) .... as a feather,
as (6) .... as a horse at the end of its tether.

As (7) .... as a church mouse, as (8) .... as muck,
as (9) .... as Chinamen dining on duck.

As (10) .... as a peacock, as (11) .... as brass,
as (12) .... as kids who are top of the class.

As (13) .... as mustard, as (14) .... as an ox,
as (15) .... as a rocker with long, filthy locks.

As (16) .... as a fiddle, as (17) .... as a rake,
as (18) .... as icing on top of a cake.

As (19) .... as the ocean, as (20) .... as time,
as (21) .... as a simile used in a rhyme.

Silly similes

The vocabulary in this poem is difficult since these are really anti-similes: the adjectives have nothing at all to do with the nouns. In fact it is a nonsense poem, in the tradition of Lewis Carroll. If I were you, I wouldn't bother about the meaning at all to start with; just let the words roll over you.

> **Vocabulary notes**
> *blunt* is the opposite of sharp (as in a knife, razor etc.);
> *cruel as a cucumber* is a variant of *cool as a cucumber* (= calm) which we met in 'Sensible Similes';
> *Michaelmas Day* is the feast day of Saint Michael, my patron saint;
> *mildew* is a disease which affects plants;
> *mutton* is sheep-meat. (the meat from a baby sheep is *lamb*);
> a *rissole* is a type of meat dish;
> a *waistcoat* is what is worn under the jacket in a three-piece suit. In the USA it is called a *vest*;
> you *weave* cloth, wool, silk etc., not pies, of course.

As fond as a finger, as safe as a spoon,
as cruel as a cucumber planted in June.

As bold as a button, as mildewed as May,
as merry as mutton from foggy Bombay.

As fast as a feather, as grand as a glove,
as weary as weather all limpid with love.

As blunt as a blazer, as clever as clay,
as ripe as a razor on Michaelmas Day.

As high as a handle, as hot as a hare,
as scarce as a scandal in Washington Square.

As lean as a lever, as silken as sighs,
as wet as a weaver of marmalade pies.

As weak as a waistcoat, as fat as a flea,
as pale as a parson from sunny Dundee.

As proud as a plum stone, as poor as a peach,
as wise as a whistle on Cheltenham beach.

As tough as a tailor, as drunk as a door,
as soft as a sailor at quarter to four.

As rich as a rissole, as dense as a duck,
as sad as a simile down on its luck.

From 'Sky in the Pie' by Roger McGough

This section ends with two poems which are full of similes.

Vocabulary notes

keen has two meanings: **1** 'enthusiastic, eager'. **2** 'sharp, harsh' like the wind; a *nib* is the sharp end of a pen; *scaffolding* is the metal frame put outside a building when you are repairing it; a *fib* is a little lie; a *lolly-ice* (usually = ice-lolly) is mainly frozen water with a bit of sugar and flavouring; a ✓ is called a *tick* (and is the sign which British teachers put on written work to show that something is correct).

The writer of this poem
Is taller than a tree
As keen as the North wind
As handsome as can be

As bold as a boxing–glove
As sharp as a nib
As strong as scaffolding
As tricky as a fib

As smooth as a lolly-ice
As quick as a lick
As clean as a chemist-shop
As clever as a ✓

The writer of this poem
Never ceases to amaze
He's one in a million billion
(or so the poem says!)

Descriptive word rhythm by Martin Glynn

Vocabulary note

mash, in West Indian English, comes from smash and means 'to harm'

Listen to the rhythm,
The sound of the word,
Flow like a river,
Fly like a bird,
Sting like a nettle,
Bite like a flea,
Smooth as your skin,
Rough like the sea,
Cold as an icicle,
Hot like the sun,
Words are static,
sometimes they run.
Noisy as thunder,
Cool like rain,
Makes you relax,
Mash your brain,
Sharp as a needle,
Solid like a rock,
Repeating like an echo,
Rhythmic as a clock,
Dangerous as a lion,
Loud as a plane,
Quiet as a whisper,
Burning like a flame,
Fast as a car,
Slow as a snail,
Rapid like a heartbeat,
Hanging like a nail,
Painful as a scratch,
Enjoyable like your food,
Horrible like your medicine,
Changing like your mood,
Tasty like a mango,
Bitter like a lime,
Soft as a coconut,
Endless as time,
Rocks you like reggae,
Sad like the blues,
Tired as a marathon,
Informs like the news,

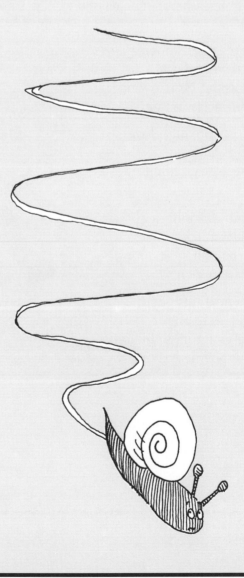

Wild as a hurricane,
Gentle as a breeze,
Irritating as a cough,
Funny as a sneeze,
Lively as a child,
Romantic like me,
Harsh like the winter,
Buzzing like a bee.

Goodbye from the rhythms,
the words and the rhyme.
Use the rhythm, check the rhythm,
It's the sign of the rhyme.

B Sayings and proverbs

English, like all languages, has a large number of sayings and proverbs. And many of them are rhythmic and often contain alliteration and rhymes.

Task fifty-six

Listen to the following and then match them with the explanations.

  1 Their bark is worse than their bite.
  2 A bird in the hand is worth two in the bush.
  3 It's no use crying over spilt milk.
  4 Too many cooks spoil the broth.
  5 A stitch in time saves nine.
  6 There's many a slip twixt (= between) cup and lip.
  7 All that glitters is not gold.
  8 Don't count your chickens before they're hatched.
  9 Least said, soonest mended.
10 Easy come, easy go.
11 Birds of a feather flock together.
12 To put the cart before the horse.
13 To put the cat among the pigeons.
14 When the cat's away the mice will play.
15 The pot calling the kettle black.
16 Two heads are better than one.
17 To make a mountain out of a molehill.
18 Don't put all your eggs in one basket.
19 Give them an inch, they'll take a mile.
20 Better be safe than sorry.

a) People with similar tastes and interests tend to meet up.

b) Remedy any slight defects early before things start to get really bad.

c) Unsupervised people are likely to misbehave.

d) It is best not to be too optimistic about the outcome of your projects.

e) Things acquired with little effort are likely to be just as easily lost.

f) You are more likely to make the correct decision having asked for a second opinion.

g) To get your priorities wrong.

h) They are likely to take advantage if you make the slightest concession.

i) They sound more threatening than they actually are.

j) There is no point complaining about past events which cannot be changed.

k) To stir up trouble deliberately.

l) Pay more attention to what you have than to what you might possibly have.

m) Do not be fooled by outward appearances.

n) To make too much of something rather trivial.

o) Caution is often the best approach.

p) 'No comment' may well be the wisest choice.

q) It can be unwise to have too many people collaborating on a project.

r) Things can go wrong, even at the very last moment.

s) Accusing someone of a defect that you also have.

t) It's best not to pin your hopes on a single person or project.

C Doubling up sounds

English is full of phrases in which sounds are doubled. This may involve:

alliteration	e.g. *spick and span / topsy turvey / head over heels*
rhyme	e.g. *doom and gloom / namby pamby / funny money*
vowel change alone	e.g. *mish mash / zig zag / criss cross / tittle tattle*

A surprising number of such phrases start with the letter 'h' (corresponding to the sound /h/). Here is the selection of them.

Task fifty-seven

Listen to them, then see if you can match them with the definitions.

1 hale and hearty (*adj*)	**a)** (done) in a great and disorganised hurry
2 hanky panky (*noun*)	**b)** breathing noisily
3 helter skelter (*adv*)	**c)** any way possible, including dishonest means
4 higgledy piggledy (*adj/adv*)	**d)** noisy activity
5 high and mighty (*adj*)	**e)** in disorder; mixed together any old how
6 hurly burly (*noun*)	**f)** very healthy and active
7 hocus pocus (*noun*)	**g)** cheating or deceit or sexually improper behaviour of a not very serious kind
8 hoi polloi (*noun*)	**h)** fine, OK
9 head over heels (*adj*)	**i)** noisy talk or fuss about something unimportant
10 huffing and puffing (*vb*)	**j)** disorder
11 (by) hook or by crook (*adv*)	**k)** too ordinary; without variety or change
	l) a number of things mixed up without any sensible order or arrangement
12 hooray Henry (*noun*)	**m)** too proud and certain of one's own importance
13 hunky dory (*adj*)	**n)** the ordinary people
14 hugger mugger (*adj/adv/phr*)	**o)** a loud-mouthed, empty-headed upper-class man
15 hot spot (*noun*)	**p)** to have a pleasant social relationship, often with someone in a higher social position
16 hot pot (*noun*)	**q)** a place where there is likely to be a lot of trouble
17 hotch potch (*noun*)	**r)** completely, uncontrollably
18 hoo-ha (*noun*)	**s)** a mutton, potato and onion stew
19 humdrum (*adj*)	**t)** the use of tricks to deceive
20 hob-nob (*vb*)	

Task fifty-eight

Fill each gap in the following sentences with one of the phrases from Task fifty-seven.

1 He's not very fit, poor man. He was .... just 10 minutes after the start of the match..
2 In cheap supermarkets they often pile up things all .... instead of putting them neatly on the shelves.
3 He's gone all .... since he got that new job. Won't have anything to do with his old friends.
4 They hardly ever go out; never been abroad. A pretty .... life altogether, if you ask me.
5 I'll get my own back on them ....
6 I hear the vicar's been up to a bit of .... with someone in the choir!
7 They couldn't cope in the .... of life.
8 How's things? Everything .... ?

Finally, to end the book, here are two nonsense sequences using a number of doubled-up phrases. Look up the meanings in a good dictionary, if you want to. But if I were you, I would just do as I have suggested before; enjoy the magic of sounds, and listen to the rhythm and music of the language.

hanky panky	tall and lanky
hale and hearty	arty farty
hubble bubble	toil and trouble
hurdy gurdy	rather wordy
hurly burly	short and curly
hocus pocus	out of focus
hunky dory	thirteenth story
helter skelter	gimme shelter

see saw	hee haw
knick knack	tick tack
mish mash	splish splash
flip flop	tip top
chitter chatter	pitter patter
ping pong	ding dong
hi fi	bye bye

Teacher's Notes

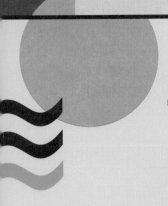

Teacher's Notes

General points

The prime function of *Rhymes and Rhythm* is to make learners of English more aware of what really happens in normal speech. This means that there is really only one thing that you must **not** do when using this material: namely, try to slow things down when repeating or asking your pupils (or students) to repeat. This is because the things that happen in normal speech happen **because of** the speed. If you slow a sequence down too much, then the various phenomena (especially elision and assimilation) just don't occur. So, if your class finds a particular sequence a bit too difficult, then **break** it down rather than **slow** it down. Do some back-chaining, for example, as I suggest as a preparation for *Chinatown* (see page 86). And you may find it useful occasionally to replace the real words by the DAH du du technique (see page 10, for an example).

That apart, feel free to experiment with the material; you know the level of your own class better than anyone else, after all. So, in the case of a gap-fill poem, for example, you can do any of the following: allocate more or fewer words for them to choose from: spend more (or less) time on pre-vocabulary work; use the poem as a dictation (by you or by members of the class); ask them to learn all or part off by heart; devise follow-up activities such as discussions, pieces of writing, and so on and so forth.

It can be a good idea to introduce a poem or chant through some choral repetition. And you don't have to start off by repeating whole lines. Take *Names*, for example (page 20). I first get them to repeat **pairs** of names:

Norman, **Mart**in (Norman, Martin) **Char**ley, **Les**ley (Charley, Lesley)

then **four** names:

Norman, **Mart**in, **Char**ley, **Les**ley (Norman, Martin, Charley, Lesley)

Then I do the same with the place names, for example:

Nottingham, **Mot**tingham, **Che**ster, **Lee** (Nottingham, Mottingham, Chester, Lee)
Jarrow, **Har**row, **Lei**cester, Dundee (Jarrow, Harrow, Leicester, Dundee)

Use this technique whenever you want to concentrate on a given type of item or stress pattern. In *Where do you think you're going?* (page 21), for example, you can practice:

conf**e**tti, spa**ghe**tti, li**bre**tto, stil**e**tto
prof**e**ssor, conf**e**ssor, com**pu**ter, com**mu**ter

You can even experiment with different **chunks** of text. Take *Arthur bought an armful of artichokes*. Before dealing with entire lines I loosen the class up by having them clap and chant sequences such as:

CLAP   CLAP   CLAP   CLAP

an **arm**ful, a **ba**rrelful, a **ki**lo, a **sack** (repeat)
an **arm**ful, an **arm**ful, an **arm**ful of **ar**tichokes (repeat)
a **ba**rrelful, a **ba**rrelful, a **ba**rrelful of **beans** (repeat)
a **ki**lo, a **ki**lo, a **ki**lo of **ca**bbages (repeat)
a **jar**, a **jar**, a **gi**ant jar of **jam** (repeat)
a **large**, a **large**, a **large** leg of **lamb** (repeat)

You will see that I use a number of conventions in the book to indicate relative degrees of stress. I suggest that you do likewise, at the very least by adopting a class convention for indicating the place of major stress in any word that they write down, maybe a little square above the relevant syllable. You expect them, after all, to get the spelling right; well, the place of main stress is just as important when they speak as is the correct spelling when they write.

And be prepared to break conventions when you write on the board. Make sure they know that we don't talk about *bananas*, for example; what we talk about are

ba**na**nas

And get in the habit of using all kinds of physical means to indicate aspects of the reality of speech. Stretch (or rather s t r e t c h) your hands apart like a concertina to show a long vowel; use a curving-down movement of the hand to show a falling tonic syllable, as in the first syllable of Chinatown, for example;

C h
    i
      i
        i na town

What I do not say is that all learners should learn to write in phonetic notation. It is used in the book a lot, of course, but mainly as a means of raising awareness, in particular of the way the schwa dominates the system of English. All the learner really needs is to be able to recognise the schwa when looking up words in a dictionary as well as the convention for distinguishing degrees of stress.

Suggestions for follow-up or related activities

Linking – Billy yate a napple ... (pages 15 and 16)

I have made a special overhead transparency to introduce this. At the top you have:

Billy ate an apple,	Billy yate a napple,
a nice ripe apple,	a nice ri papple.
Lucy ate an ice cream	Lucy yate a ni scream,
a nice creamy ice cream	a nice creamy yice cream

I reveal first Billy ate an apple, then Billy yate a napple, saying 'this is how it's written ... and this is how it's actually said'. The rest of the sheet consists of prompts such as:

Beattie	orange	juicy
Flo	apricot	yellow
Sally	onion	Spanish

At first I cover up the adjectives, revealing just the name and thing to eat. These prompts lead to the first, short chant: *Beattie ate an orange, Flo ate an apricot, Sally ate an onion*, etc. Then I hide the names while revealing the column of adjectives, which leads to a chant of *a nice juicy orange, a nice yellow apricot, a nice Spanish onion*, and so on. Finally, all is revealed and we end up with the full chant, as it is written in the book: *Beattie ate an orange, a nice juicy orange, Flo ate an apricot, a nice yellow apricot*, etc.

And what kind of summer did **you** have (pages 16-18)

If you have access to a big map or an atlas, it's a good idea to trace the route around Europe and North Africa.

You can also ask them to match other place names to the stress patterns. e.g.

■ ○	Cairo Lima Warsaw Moscow
○ ■	Belgrade Berlin Rangoon
○ ■ ○	Caracas Havana Jakarta Djibouti Damascus
● ○ ■	Bucharest

Where do you think you're going? (pages 20-22)

Note how many nouns with the pattern ○ ■ ○:

a) are borrowed from other languages – Latin, Spanish and Italian in particular;

b) end with a written vowel, especially <a>, <o> or <i>;

c) have schwa (or occasionally short /ɪ/) in the first syllable.

Examples include:

banana / vanilla / saliva / potato / tobacco / libretto / spaghetti / salami

Now look at some of the many 4-syllable nouns which come from the same languages and have the same endings:

influenza / diarrhoea / california / impetigo / sostenuto / avocado / armadillo / macaroni / fettucini

Each has main stress on the third syllable, secondary stress on the first, and weak second and final syllables, often with schwa.

In other words, there are rules determining how we oblige loan-words of these types to conform to the English system. Because of this I have simple code names for them; I call such 3-syllable nouns 'banana words' and such 4-syllable nouns 'avocado words'. This acts as a quick reminder to my students of the powerful patterning that affects these words.

In fact it would make sense to have a number of words which act as permanent reminders of the most powerful patterns. You could have an area set aside in the classroom for these reminder words, something like this perhaps:

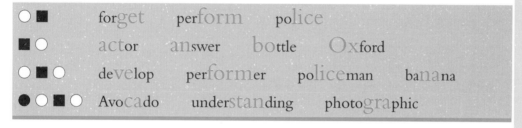

You could put words/ patterns up as you draw the attention of the class towards them. For example, the pattern ■ ○ ○ might not be needed until you drew their attention to words such as photograph and microphone. Once the key words are up – the template words if you like – then they can be referred to when a member of the class has a problem with a word the stessing of which is predictable.

Alliteration – Names (pages 19 and 20)

Alliteration – the use of recurring initial consonant sounds – can make is easier to memorise both verse and prose. But you shouldn't overdo things: piling on multiple examples of the same sound in rapid sequence can make things worse. So be careful of tongue-twisters such as 'round the rugged rocks the ragged rascal ran' or 'Peter Piper picked a peck of pickled pepper'; they are likely to cause great confusion and create inhibitions when the sound is encountered later by the learner.

I have tried to avoid such pitfalls in this section. In Names the sounds come in pairs, which seems to be the best way to start. And the use of names – whether of people or places – cuts down on problems of meaning, allowing the learner to concentrate on the rhythm (in this case, a fast waltz time: ONE two three, ONE two three).

A creative way to use this poem is to give out verses 1 and 5. You then supply a jumbled list of the personal and place names. Their task is firstly, to match up the rhyming place names (Stratford/Catford, Cork/York, etc.), and then to reconstruct the missing verses by matching, say, Stephen or Stanley to Stratford, Colin, Cora or Cuthbert to Catford, and so on. Note that it doesn't matter if the pairings are different from the original, provided that they match in terms of alliteration.

Two-part alliteration (pages 22 and 23)

The *do-it-yourself tongue-twister kit* (as its name implies) allows the class to build their own sequences, starting at elementary level with just two sound repetitions and leading gradually up to five.

I start this off by a class game – suitable at any level – which acts as an ear-training activity as well as a vocabulary test. This is the way it goes:

1 Show them (on an OHT, or written on the board) the following three sentences:

   a) Kenneth bought some carrots.

   b) Polly bought some peaches

   c) Shirley bought some sugar

   Ask the class what each has in common. They may mention the structure, the rhythm or whatever, but persist until someone points out that it is the initial **sound**. (Not the initial **letter**; that's why I use *Kenneth* and *cabbage*.)

2 Replace the example with:

   a) Kenneth bought some carrots.

   b) Cathy bought some carrots.

   c) Carol bought some carrots.

   and this time ask how they are different. Someone will eventually realise that in a) there is only one initial sound in common, the consonant, but that b) has two, /k/ + /æ/, and c) has four, /k/ + /æ/ + /r/ + /ə/.

3 Divide the class into groups, allocating each a piece of chalk and some board space. Their task is to write up as many pairs as possible in the time allowed them, for example, *Ben/bananas*; *Sally/sandwiches*; *Tom/tea*. (The second word must be buyable). Before they start writing you should tell them that a *Kenneth/carrots* choice can win them 1 point, a *Cathy/carrots* choice 2 points, and so on. You then start them off, your task being to stop any group using a word that has already been written up.

4 Finally, you come to the most interesting part, where each team has to say how many points they think they deserve. Have an individual read out one pair, then you repeat it clearly and loudly, two or three times if the pronunciation needs correcting. The student then has to say how many points the pair deserves. A correct choice wins that number of points for the team; but an incorrect choice means no points. (Typical examples of ill-judged choices include: expecting more than 1 point for *Tom/tomato* or *Barbara/banana*; or being misled by the spelling into choosing *Susan/sugar* or *Sheila/sandwiches*.)

Three-part alliteration (pages 23-25)

You introduce the third element through a few examples, such as, *Kenneth bought a kilo of carrots / Polly bought a packet of peanuts / Gerry bought a jar of jam.*

Explain that they can write similar sequences by using:

- a **container** (*sack, cup, mug, bag, tin, jar, ...*)

- an **amount** (*pound, metre, yard, ton, gram, ...*)

- a word ending in **-ful** (*armful, mouthful, handful, fistful, ...*)

- an appropriate word followed by **full** (*a room full of ... a lorry full of ...*)

If they are advanced enough they will be able to produce their own examples, otherwise this is an appropriate time to introduce new vocabulary. But now that you have reached three repetitions you should expect no more than the initial sound to be common to all three words.

The *Arthur bought an armful of artichokes* poem can usefully be introduced at this stage. Its driving beat will force the class to concentrate on the stressed syllables in the lexical items, without allowing them time to linger over the others. (Remember that too slow a delivery will make the weak vowels artificially strong!)

Then, if the class is advanced enough, you can ask them to come up with the alternatives to *bought* and the alliterative adjectives found in the later part of the section. Remember that the whole sequence can be spread over weeks, or indeed months, and referred to whenever the class has reached an appropriate level of vocabulary.

Stress in verbs and nouns

The general rule that 2-syllable verbs tend to have front stress (i.e. ○ ■) and 2-syllable nouns the reverse, is extremely powerful. You will do your pupils a service if they are made aware of this from the very beginning. Two sequences are particularly useful if you want the reader to concentrate on the difference between initial stressed and unstressed syllables, namely: (page 33) *Conrad composed a concerto for trumpet* and (pages 39 and 40) *Who's who.*

The first contains a sequence of 2-syllable names with front stress: *Percy, Colin, Betty, Annie, Debbie*, and so on. These contrast with a number of 2-syllable verbs starting with a weakly-stressed syllable **usually represented by the same letters as the name**: *persuade, conduct, behave, announce, devote.*

The second adopts a similar approach, but this time the weak first syllables are found in nouns **derived from verbs**, which gives such contrastive pairs as:*Col / collector; Con / confessor; Sol / solicitor.*

Who's who (pages 39 and 40)?

Where possible it is a good idea to combine work on pronunciation with that on other levels of language, vocabulary in particular. With this poem I often play what I call a 'Definition game'. You divide the class into groups of appropriate size. They choose four or five nouns and work out definitions for them. Each group gives its definition and the others try to be the first to guess which noun is being defined. Points are allocated on a scale of 1-3 for imaginative definitions. (Thus in the case of *whaler* you would give 1 point for '*a person who catches whales*'; 2 points for '*a person who hunts large mammals which live in the sea*', maybe 3 for '*this is a job that many people think shouldn't exist*' which came up in one of my classes. Similarly, you allocate points for the answers; 2 for the correct one, 1 for others which can be justified (or 2 for imaginative justifications, as in the case of the group which claimed that teachers shouldn't exist).

A moral tale (page 44)

This can be expanded into a story, written by students individually or in groups. What actually happened to the person? What went wrong? It can be written from the point of view of the person concerned or someone else involved as a newspaper article, or even as an obituary.

Task eighteen (pages 51 and 52)

Remember that the place of main stress is also the place of the **tonic syllable**. This means that in the sentence *She was wearing a cotton dress* the voice does its final fall on dress. By contrast in *They work in a cotton factory* the final fall is on the first syllable of *cotton*, with the remaining syllables at the bottom of the voice. For example:

Old and new information (page 61)

Here is another way to practice the shift from a **fall-rise** (for old information) to a **fall** (for new information).

Take a passage or story with which the class are already familiar, then recite it with a few deliberate mistakes. You train them to point out and correct your mistake. With *Little Red Riding Hood*, for example, you could say:

Teacher:	One day, little Blue **Ri**ding Hood woke up and ...
Student (interrupts):	Not little **Blue** Riding Hood, little **Red** Riding Hood!
Teacher:	That's right, sorry. Alright then. One day, little Red Riding Hood woke up and her Mummy said to her, 'would you take these cakes to your **Grand**father, he's very sick.'

> Student (interrupts): Not her Grand**father**, her Grand**mo**ther!
> Teacher: Yes, of course, so Little Red Riding Hood took the basket of cakes and drove off down the road … etc.
> Student (interrupts): She didn't **drive**, she went on **foot**!

Have you seen Peter? (pages 73 and 74)

This is a good opportunity for pupils to try their hands at some simple poetry. Give them just a few examples of both versions, then provide a few pairs of names: *William + Bill / Susan + Sue / Patricia + Pat*, for example. It is up to them to complete the couplets.

Down the Diner (pages 79 and 80)

Before doing the dictation get them to call out, then write up on the board, various types of food that they think might be on the menu in a diner in the USA. With a little patience you can often elicit most of the items on the menu. If such items are not in their vocabulary, then you have to pre-teach them, of course.

When I dictate this piece I often break the phrases down into chunks in the way I suggested earlier for *Arthur bought an armful of artichokes*. For example:

> a **rack** or two, a **rack** or two, a **rack** or two of **ribs**
> = ə 'rækə tuː ə 'rækə tuː ə 'rækə tuː ə 'rɪbz
>
> a **chi**cken, a **chi**cken, a **sou**thern fried **chi**cken

Rapping the rules (pages 89 and 90)

I have this written out on two OHTs (two, because the words would be too small if it was put on one). And I present it using a technique which I call '*OHT Striptease*'. This means covering up much of the text, asking the class to guess what is coming next, and only revealing it letter by letter. Take the third line. If you reveal only:

If you don't want your English to sound …

then what follows could indeed be a **noun** phrase, as in the case. But it could also be an **adjective** or adjectival phrase (*quite odd / real strange*). So you accept such suggestions as reasonable, **then** reveal the next word, giving:

If you don't want your English to sound a …

Now it must be a noun phrase, but could equally be *a muddle*, for example. In the next you give them:

You've got to hit the …

If someone says *stress*, point out you need it for the rhyme, and play the first couplet to remind them of the rhythm (and hence the line length). If nobody guesses beat, then reveal it letter by letter until they do:

hit the b… hit the be… hit the bea…

As you go on, you can expect more from them. Get them to complete the similes in Rule 2, for example:

And words go together like ...
And words go together like links ...
They follow each other like ...

(The second line is easier to complete, since by them they know it must rhyme with *chain*).

Part Four – Playing with Poems (page 92)

Pay special attention to the points made on page 92, in connection with the poem *Going Shopping*. Don't concentrate so much on stress and rhythm that you end up with a class producing impeccably stressed but machine-like English. The music of English is as important as the rhythm.

Song for London (pages 105-107)

This topic lends itself to discussion/debate activities. I divide the class into *Good News* and *Bad News* groups. The first collect the advantages of living in a big city, the second the disadvantages. (Choose a specific city, or cities in general).

Failure (page 108)

If your class still have problems with pronouncing final *-ed* in past participles, then this poem will help.

/t/	fished / smashed / crashed
/d/	studied / learned / proved / trained / aimed / transferred / lied / played / opened / turned / married / joined
/ɪd/	decided / landed / invested / collected / wounded / hunted / potted

On your bike (pages 124 and 125)

Here's another one which lends itself to discussion. In this case I divide them into groups of **motorists**, **cyclists** and **pedestrians**. The activity is in two parts. First, they collect all the bad things they can say about the other groups and then start a slanging match, e.g.

● Why don't you cyclists ever look where you're going?

● Us! Well **you** can talk! You never even notice us!

When they have got really heated I tell them to calm down and get together to think of ways things can be improved (special cycle lanes, underpasses etc.).

As (page 132)

You can make this into an exercise by supplying them with the adjectives and nouns separately. Thus:

black / dead / dry / free / hard / heavy / light / live / plain / plump / poor / rough / soft / steady / strong / tight / uncertain / weak / wet / white / the air / a bear / a bird / a bone / a cat / coal / a drum / a feather / a fish / flint / a horse / lead / a lily / a mole / a partridge / a pikestaff / a rat / stone / time / weather

The exercise is in four parts.

1   They try to complete the similes: *as black as coal.*

2   Then they match the rhymes: *as black as coal / as soft as a mole.*

3   Bearing in mind that the rhyming words end each line, they match the internal oppositions: *as white a a lily / as black as coal.*

4   Finally, they complete the full poem. (The couplets can have their lines either way round, of course.)

Keys to the tasks

KEYS TO THE TASKS

Task one

biology (4)	bridge (1)	strength (1)	photographer (4)
watches (2)	unabridged (3)	support (2)	jumped (1)
jumpers (2)	policeman (3)	decided (3)	obeyed (2)

Task two

	1 syllable	2 syllables	3 syllables	4 syllables
Cities	Leith	Cardiff	Manchester	W'hampton
Boys' names	George	Peter	Anthony	Alexander
Girls' names	Ann	Janet	Jemima	Felicity
Animals	bear	giraffe	elephant	rhinoceros
Countries	Spain	Japan	Morocco	Afghanistan
Rivers	Nile	Volga	Amazon	Mississippi

Task three

	■○○	○■○	○○■
Manchester	Manchester		
Anthony	Anthony		
Jemima		Jemima	
elephant	elephant		
Morocco		Morocco	
Amazon	Amazon		

Task four

	○ ■ ○ ○	○ ○ ■ ○
Felicity	Felicity	
Afghanistan	Afghanistan	
Alexander		Alexander
Wolverhampton		Wolverhampton
rhinoceros	rhinoceros	
Mississippi		Mississippi

Task five

grow(er)   yellow   a(l)oud   hunted   f(or)give   photo

Tim(o)thy   Germ(a)ny   ban(a)na(s)   workm(a)nship   t(o)morrow

(Eliz)abeth   Arg(entina)   phot(o)graph   phot(o)gra(ph)y   ph(o)tographic

Note: *Elizabeth* can start with short /ɪ/ or with schwa. And do not worry about the change of stress and of vowels in *photograph*, *photographic* and *photography*. The stress pattern of these, and of other words, is rule-based, as we shall see.

Task six

This is **the** house **that** Jack built.
ˈðɪs ɪz ðə ˈhaʊs ðət ˈdʒæk ˈbɪlt
These **are the** houses **that** Jack built.
ˈðiːz ə ðə ˈhaʊsɪz ðət ˈdʒæk ˈbɪlt
Those **are the** people we drove **to the** party.
ˈðəʊz ə ðə ˈpiːpəl wi ˈdrəʊv tə ðə ˈpɑːti
That is **the** gardener who works **for** my mother.
ˈðæt ɪz ðə ˈgɑːdnə huː ˈwɜːks fə maɪ ˈmʌðə
Andrew is taller **than** Peter **and** Thomas.
ˈændruːʷ ɪz ˈtɔːlə ðən ˈpiːtər ən ˈtɒməs
Fancy **a** glass **of** Italian brandy?
ˈfænsiʲ ə ˈglɑːs əv ɪˈtæljən ˈbrændi
Tom's not **as** tall **as the** rest **of the** family.
ˈtɒmz nɒt əz ˈtɔːl əz ðə ˈrest ə(v) ðə ˈfæməli
What **an** amazingly lively production.
ˈwɒt ən əˈmeɪzɪŋli ˈlaɪvli prəˈdʌkʃən

Task seven
a)

■	○ ■	■ ○	○ ■ ○	● ○ ■ ○
Rome	Madrid	Brussels	Valetta	Algeciras
Cannes	Toulouse	Lisbon	Granada	Casablanca
Spain	Algiers	Brisbane	Verona	
France	Tangier	Malta	Gibraltar	
Sfax		Tunis	Morocco	
		Venice	Pamplona	

b) The odd one out is Santander = ● ○ ■

Task eight
The following place names always have schwa:

Ventnor   *Plymouth*   *Poland*
ˈventnə   ˈplɪməθ   ˈpəʊlənd

Brighton is either ˈbraɪtən (with schwa) or ˈbraɪtn, with /n/ as syllabic consonant.

The rest are pronounced as follows: *Stockport* = ˈstɒkpɔːt; *Stockholm* = ˈstɒkhəʊm; *Stansted* = ˈstænsted; *Soho* = ˈsəʊhəʊ

Task nine
The following definitely have schwa in the first syllable:

bananas vanilla salami pastrami confetti spaghetti professor confessor baloney computer commuter

The following have schwa in the **second** syllable, not the first.

sarsparilla = ˌsɑːspəˈrɪlə; macaroni = ˌmækəˈrəʊni

The following usually has schwa in the first syllable, though some people use /ɪ/:

pyjamas = pəˈdʒɑːməz or pɪˈdʒɑːməz

The following usually have /ɪ/ in the first syllable, though some people use schwa:

relation   libretto   stiletto

Task ten
The ones ending in <-a>, <-er> and <-or>:

banana(s)   pyjama(s)   vanilla   sarsparilla   professor   confessor
computer   commuter

note that *people* and *steeple* may either end in /əl/ or with syllabic /l/

Task eleven

provide	supply	collect	promote	consult	confuse
prə'vaid	sə'plai	kə'lekt	prə'məʊt	kən'sʌlt	kən'fjuːz

reform and *secure* usually have /ɪ/ in the first syllable, though some people use schwa.

Task twelve

1 e)	6 b)	11 d)	16 n)
2 i)	7 r)	12 g)	17 a)
3 m)	8 k)	13 s)	18 o)
4 l)	9 j)	14 p)	19 c)
5 h)	10 f)	15 t)	20 q)

Note: the adjectives *artful*, *sly* and *tricky* are fairly close in meaning. Look them up in a very good monolingual dictionary.

Task thirteen

1 g)	7 w)	13 o)	19 l)
2 p)	8 s)	14 k)	20 v)
3 j)	9 b)	15 t)	21 c)
4 f)	10 d)	16 h)	22 n)
5 e)	11 a)	17 x)	23 u)
6 m)	12 q)	18 i)	24 r)

Task fourteen

1 surprise	2 develop	3 reload	4 introduce
collect	abolish	pre-set	contradict
defend	consider	defuse	overwhelm
prefer	surrender	co-chair	undertake
refuse	determine	prepaint	interfere
remove	enliven	demist	understand

5 tremble	6 estimate	7 realise
wander	clarify	circularise
soften	substitute	apologise
damage	accelerate	monopolise
measure	occupy	sentimentalise
worry	identify	idolise

Task fifteen

1 g)	5 j)	9 c)	13 i)
2 p)	6 k)	10 n)	14 b)
3 a)	7 m)	11 o)	15 d)
4 e)	8 f)	12 h)	16 l)

Task sixteen

a) *selector*, *diver*, *confessor*, *translator* and *teacher* all derive from verbs and keep the stress of the original verb (*doctor*, *barrister*, *tailor* and *broker* do not derive from verbs).

b) *airman*, like *chairman*, is a compound noun composed of two elements, with stress on the first element – see section C.

c) *democrat* and *cosmonaut* are both composed of two classical elements, with stress on first syllable – see section C.

d) *musician*, like *physician* (and most words ending in <ian> or <ion>, has the stress falling on the syllable before the end – see B 4a).

e) *photographer*, *zoologist*, *geographer* and *philanthropist* all end with a ■ ○ ○ suffix and are derived from <-y> nouns – see B 4c).

f) *idealist*, *loyalist* and *realist* all derive from adjectives, with no change of stress – see B 4g), (*balloonist* derives from a noun, not an adjective).

g) *neurotic* like *psychotic*, ends with a suffix that imposes stress on the preceding syllable – see B 4f).

Odd ones out:
hack (= insulting term for a journalist) is a monosyllable, and *poet* fits none of the categories.

Task seventeen

1 p)	8 b)	15 n)	22 u)
2 h)	9 c)	16 v)	23 o)
3 y)	10 g)	17 t)	24 f)
4 q)	11 j)	18 d)	25 l)
5 a)	12 r)	19 bb)	26 w)
6 s)	13 aa)	20 x)	27 m)
7 z)	14 e)	21 i)	28 k)

Task eighteen

Phrases

a cotton 'dress	= a dress which is made of cotton
rubber 'gloves	= gloves which are made of rubber
a meat 'pie	= a pie which is made of meat
an English 'teacher	= a teacher who is English
a black 'bird	= a bird which is black
that white 'house	= that house which is white

a moving 'train	= a train which is moving	
the winning 'horse	= the horse which won the race	

Compounds

a 'cotton factory	= a factory where cotton is made
a 'rubber plant	= a type of plant
a 'meat packer	= a packer of meat / person who packs meat
an 'English teacher	= a teacher of English / person who teaches
a 'blackbird.	= a type of bird
the 'white House	= a particular house where the US President lives
a 'moving van	= a van used for moving furniture etc.
the 'winning post	= the post which shows where the race ends

Task nineteen

Compounds

earrings   tennis shoes   riding breeches   evening gown   handbag
overcoats   underwear

Phrases

cotton skirt   leather belt   silken blouses   linen shirt   flashy scarf
summer blouses   winter hose   cashmere sweaters   cheapish dress

Task twenty

1 through stopped Vaughan knives
2 hungry leather follow Michael Leicester
3 Peru Iran a few police defend Macbeth
4 dead drunk red hot tired out next year buy now
5 somebody Hungary sympathy Manchester after it
6 tomato Madonna policeman embargo a big one Trafalgar
7 to the school for a while as a rule
8 best results half a pound outer space Charing Cross
9 photographic institution Speaker's Corner inner circle Nelson's Column
   buy a new one half a sandwich
10 give me a drink Madam Tussaud's Royal Exchange buy us some food
   go to the bank
11 biology maternity the last of them conservative a pound of it Elizabeth
12 come to the disco geriatrician Kensington High Street offer him money
   try a banana Buckingham Palace
13 biographical Peter Davidson disability
14 sending a telegram autobiography all of the elephants

Task twenty-one

one night stand	a long-haired drummer	a rock 'n' roll band
a four-hour show	a first-rate gig	a well-earned hand
a red-headed woman	high-heeled shoes	a bald-headed fellow
an unnamed fan	stone-cold sober	absolutely grand
instrumental numbers	rock 'n' roll licks	bass-drum pedal

Task twenty-two

In the fast version the final consonant of the numeral or adjective disappeared: the /t/ in *first*, *next* and *last*; and the /d/ in *second* and *third*.

The firs(t) girl and the firs(t) boy
The secon(d) girl and the secon(d) boy
The thir(d) girl and the thir(d) boy
The nex(t) girl and the nex(t) boy
The las(t) girl and the las(t) boy

Task twenty-three

The /n/ of *secon(d) girl* changes to /ŋ/ (the sound at the end of *thing*, *song* etc.)
The /n/ of *secon(d) boy* changes to /m/
The /d/ of *third girl* changes to /g/
The /d/ of *third boy* changes to /b/

Task twenty-four

2 a perfec(t) morning
3 perfec(t)ly marvellous
5 she wan(t)s ten poun(d)s of butter
6 he fin(d)s it boring
7 have the fac(t)s as soon as possible
8 I watch(ed) four differen(t) programmes las(t) night
9 Jane hates fas(t) food so she won('t) want any burgers
10 We're having roas(t) beef with bake(d) potatoes an(d) beans

Task twenty-five

Elision of /d/ or /t/ is not possible in:

● *hardware*, *word perfect* and *smart card*; <r> is not a spoken consonant, so /d/ and /t/ follow a vowel sound.

● *loud speaker* /d/ follows a vowel sound

● *turned off* /d/ is followed by a vowel sound

● Note that the /d/ of *word perfect* and the /t/ of *smart card* may both change (i.e. may be assimilated).

Task twenty-six

2 glad / sad / mad / bad
3 well / swell (you can look like hell = 'in a bad way').
4 glum (= 'sad') / numb (= unable to feel, from shock etc.)
5 fat (a person can't be flat)
6 sick (you can't look quick; a person can look thick = 'appear stupid', but that means permanently)
7 smart
8 shy / sly (possibly high, too = 'under the influence of drugs')
9 slim / grim (= angry, in a bad mood)
10 thin

11 great
12 fine
13 blue (= sad)

Task twenty-seven

When /n/ does not change

The sound /n/ is an alveolar nasal, i.e. a nasal produced with the tongue touching the tooth ridge. If the next sound is also produced with the tongue in the same general area, then the transition from one sound to the next is easy. This is the case when /n/ is followed by /d/, /t/, /s/, /ʃ/, /θ/, /r/ and /l/, which explains why *ten* does not change in such contexts as: *ten dogs, ten downs, ten truths, ten sighs, ten saucers, ten shouts, ten things, ten rings, ten lies.*

When /n/ can change

1 /n/ can become the **bilabial** nasal /m/ before any other bilabials (i.e. sounds which involve closing of the lips).
before /b/ *ten boys, ten brooches*
before /p/ *ten pounds, ten parks, ten peaches,* ten pearls
before /m/ *ten moons, ten marks,* ten monkeys

2 /n/ can become the **velar** nasal /ŋ/ before the other two velar sounds (i.e. those where the back of the tongue touches the velum, or soft palate).
before /g/ *ten girls, ten gardens, ten grapes*
before /k/ *ten cats, ten coats, ten cups*

Task twenty-eight

Old Street	elision of /d/	ˈəʊl ˌstriːt
Holland Park	elision of /d/; /n/ becomes /m/	ˌhɒləm ˈpɑːk
Hyde Park	/d/ becomes /b/	ˌhaɪb ˈpɑːk
Old Kent Road	elision of /d/; /t/ becomes a glottal stop	ˌəʊl ˌkenʔ ˈrəʊd
Bond Street	elision of /d/	ˈbɒn ˌstriːt
Saint Paul's	elision of /t/; /n/ becomes /m/	ˌsəm ˈpɔːlz
London Bridge	/n/ becomes /m/	ˌlʌndəm ˈbrɪdʒ

Task twenty-nine

	on hands and knees	faster than walking	on one foot	no sense of hurry	usually in the country	out of control
jog		✓				
stroll				✓		
ramble					✓	
saunter				✓		
run		✓				
lurch						✓
crawl	✓					
hop			✓			
hike					✓	

Task thirty

(1) Southern fried chicken (note the elided /d/. *fried* sounds like *fry*)
(2) ham and lettuce salad (the /s/ at the end of lettuce becomes part of the /s/ in *salad*. This means it sounds like *ham and letter salad*)
(3) thousand island dressing (you hear the /d/ in *thousand* but not in *island*)
(4) blue cheese
(5) double western omelette (the /n/ of *western* links to *omelette*)
(6) sausages
(7) peas (*and peas* = əm 'piːz)
(8) rack (= the ribs are not cut off and served individually)
(9) ribs (= pork spare ribs)
(10) barbecue sauce
(11) king-size burger (= very large hamburger)
(12) ketchup (a thick, sweet tomato sauce) (the /p/ links to *of*)
(13) burger (the /r/ links to *in*)
(14) sesame bun (a bun containing sesame seeds)
(15) rump steak
(16) onions
(17) chilli (there's a /j/ link in *chilli on*)
(18) steak and mushroom (*and mushroom* = ə 'mʌʃruːm)
(19) mashed potato (the /d/ is elided, so *mashed* sounds like *mash*)
(20) French fries (usually called *chips* in Britain)
(21) salt-beef sandwich (the /t/ of *salt* becomes a glottal stop)
(22) French mustard
(23) apple pie
(24) scoops (the ice cream is scooped out with a special instrument)

(25) ice cream (the linking makes it sound like *I scream*)
(26) stack (= a little pile)
(27) pancakes (assimilation makes it sound like *pang cakes*)
(28) syrup (the /p/ links to *on*)
(29) ice cream sundae (a rich mixture of ice cream, fruit, syrup etc.)
(30) cheesecake
(31) strawberry
(32) diet coke (the /t/ becomes a glottal stop. Note that coke is a registered trade mark of the Coca Cola company)

Task thirty-one
elision
bes(t) friend   bran(d) new   secon(d)-hand   nex(t)-door   lan(d)lord

elision and possible assimilation
san(d)wiches = *sanwiches* or *samwiches*

Task thirty-two
elision
bes(t) friend   bran(d) new   secon(d)-hand   nex(t) door   poun(d)s   lan(d)lord
lan(d)lady   Chris(t)mas   las(t) week   promise(d) that   nex(t) week

elision giving rise to assimilation
han(d) bag = *hambag*   frien(d) bought = *frembought*   han(d) mack = *ham mack*
len(d) me = *lem me*   corn(ed) beef = *corm beef*   gran(d)mother = *gram mother*
cann(ed) potatoes = *cam potatoes*

assimilation
made me = *mabe me*   at Christmas = ək krɪsməs

assimilation or glottal stop
a fortnigh(t) back = *a fortnipe back* or fɔʔnaɪʔ bæk
ge(t) my bags packed = *gep my* or geʔ maɪ

/t/ = glottal stop
right now   bought me   brought me

coalescent assimilation
might use = *my choose* /maɪ tʃuːz/

Task thirty-three

	/s/	/z/		/s/	/z/
course	course		please		please
discuss	discuss		express	express	
miss	miss		revise		revise
use		use	pass	pass	
practise	practise		amaze		amaze

Of course it was those ending with /s/ which coalesced with /j/ to become /ʃ/, and those ending in /z/ which coalesced with /j/ to become /ʒ/

Task thirty-four

a) every example of **linking** in Verse 2

And words go together li**ke‿links‿in‿a** chain;
they follo**w‿each‿o**ther like waggon**s‿on‿a** train

consonant to vowel links: links in   in a   follow each   each other
waggons on   on a

consonant to consonant link: like links (sounds like 'lie clinks')

b) every example of **elision** in the introduction and Verse 5

If you wan(t) to make your English come alive,
jus(t) listen to my rules from one to five.

You're getting better now, but to be the bes(t),
jus(t) remember two soun(d)s can coalesce.

between two consonants: jus(t) listen   jus(t) remember   soun(d)s

identical sounds meeting: wan(t) to

similar sounds meeting + /t/ between two consonants: bes(t) just

c) Every example of **anticipatory assimilation** in Verses 3, 4 and 5.

Now listen really close and you will hear
that certai**n ki**nds of soun**(d) ca**n disappear.

And remember if you want to increase your range
that a sou**n(d) can m**ake another sound change.

You're getting better now, but to be the best,
just remember two sounds ca**n c**oalesce.

straight assimilation: certain kinds   can coalesce = /n/ → /ŋ/;
can make = /n/ → /m/;

assimilation following /d/ elision: soun(d) can = /n/ → /ŋ/;

d) Every example of **coalescent assimilation** in the whole rap.

If you don(t) wan**t y**our English
ɪf jʊ ˈdəʊn ˈwʌntʃə ˈrɪŋglɪʃ

Bu**t yo**u're going to soun(d) funny,
bʌtʃə ˈgəʊnə ˈsaʊn ˈfʌni

Now listen really close an**d y**ou will hear
naʊ ˈlɪsn ˈrɪəli ˈkləʊs ən ˈdʒuː wɪl hɪə

And remember if you want to increa**se y**our range
ɔn rɪˈmembərɪf jə wʌn tʊ ʷɪŋ ˈkriːʃɔː ˈreɪndʒ

/t/ + /j/ → /tʃ/: want your   but your
/d/ + /j/ → /dʒ/: and you
/s/ + /j/ → /ʃ/: increase your

Task thirty-five
1 Crewe	3 night	5 true
2 shoe	4 fright	

Task thirty-six
1 Kong	4 note	7 bell	10 tell
2 song	5 gong	8 averred	
3 wrote	6 Estelle	9 heard	

Task thirty-seven
1 Crewe	4 about	7 dine	10 nine	13 suppose
2 stew	5 too	8 eleven	11 Kent	14 nose
3 shout	6 Rhine	9 seven	12 bent	15 went

Task thirty-eight
There was a young girl in the choir
Whose voice rose up higher and higher
Till it reached such a height
It was clear out of sight
And they found it next day in the spire.

A girl who weighed many an ounce
Used language I dare not pronounce.
For a fellow, unkind,
Pulled her chair out behind
Just to see (so he said) if she'd bounce.

A certain old lady from Crewe
Once dropped her false teeth in the stew.
Said a sensitive waiter
'It's horrid to cater
For careless old people like you!'

Task thirty-nine

1 A sprightly old man from LA
2 Once said to his wife, 'If I may
3 I think I will stand
4 **on my head in the Strand,'**
5 To which she retorted: 'okay.'

6 **A greedy old grandad from Duns,**
7 Once said he'd eat ninety-nine buns.
8 At the seventy-first,
9 **He unluckily burst,**
10 So the rest were consumed by his sons.

Task forty

There was an old man of Khartoum
Who kept two tame sheep in his room.
To remind him, he said
Of two friends who were dead;
But he could not remember of whom.

A greedy young lady called Perkins
Was awfully fond of small gherkins.
She devoured forty-three
One day for her tea
And pickled her internal workings.

When the shortage of fuel made it hard,
To maintain the big blaze in our yard;
We threw on Aunt Flo,
Who heightened the glow,
But I fear she became somewhat charred.

Tasks forty-one and forty-two

(If more than one is given, the first one is the original.)

(1) useful / tiring
(2) pause
(3) daring / dangerous
(4) doors
(5) important / demanding / unusual / exhausting
(6) laws
(7) unusual / demanding (possibly important / exhausting)
(8) applause
(9) stranger / odder
(10) claws
(11) healthy / tiring / useful
(12) doors

Task forty-three

(1) famine	(7) life	(13) priest
(2) beast	(8) peace	(14) most
(3) wise	(9) thief	(15) poverty
(4) rule	(10) worry	(16) health
(5) doubt	(11) free	(17) pride
(6) silence	(12) listener	(18) side

Task forty-four

(If more than one is possible, the first is the original.)

(1) down

(2) town

(3) jump / wave / clap

(4) shout

(5) money

(6) each (*every* fits the meaning but is too long; *all* fits the metre but not the meaning)

(7) spaghetti (you can't eat *confetti*)

(8) sack / bag / pound

(9) tin / can / bit / pound / sack / bag

(10) cat

Task forty-five

(If more than one is possible, it is the first one which is the original.)

(11) beans

(12) Peter

(13) chocolate / sugar / biscuits

(14) cake

(15) pound

(16) cheese

(17) who / they

(18) crates / pounds / bags

(19) does / can

(20) meat

(21) time

(22) heating

Tasks forty-six and forty-seven

(Note that if more than one word is given then they all fit, but it is the first one which comes from the original poem.)

(1) tubes / trains (*buses* is too long)

(2) buses

(3) by / at / for

(4) leave at eight

(5) shining / rising / setting

(6) gold

(7) arrows / rainbows

(8) glad / pleased (*happy* is too long)

(9) explain

(10/11) fumes, dirt, rain (other words such as *crowds*, *smog*, *filth* etc. could also fit. If you put *fog*, then you have seen too many old Sherlock Holmes films!)

(12) lorries / buses (*cars* is too short).

(13) cycle (no, I don't *drive*, and the word's too short anyway).

(14) nightfall / midnight

(15) afraid (*frightened* is stressed on the wrong syllable, and *scared* is too short).

(16) know (you speak *to* your neighbours)

(17) after

(18) use (you *look through* a hole)

(19) at the door

(20) concert

(21) play / film

(22) tell you why

(23) die

(24) dogs

(25) dark

(26) rubbish

(27) pollution

(28) breathing / sleeping?

(29) seems to care

(30) stroll / walk

(31/32) get ... down

(33) agree

(34) though / but

(35) tired of life

Task forty-eight

2 k)/d)	5 t)/m)	8 i)/e)	11 n)/l)
3 g)/s)	6 p)/a)	9 r)/j)	
4 q)/o)	7 f)/b)	10 h)/c)	

Task forty-nine

(1) stumble	(4) train	(7) rain	(10) rumble
(2) crumble	(5) fumble	(8) brain	(11) explain
(3) again	(6) tumble	(9) jumble	

Task fifty

1 f)	4 h)	7 e)	10 a)
2 d)	5 g)	8 i)	
3 j)	6 c)	9 b)	

Task fifty-one

shattered = broken into very small pieces (glass, crockery etc.)
tattered = old and torn (clothing, flags etc.)
slashed = cut with long violent strokes (people, vegetation, prices etc.)
gashed = cut very deeply (skin, wood etc.)

Task fifty-two

A suggested / congested / rested / tested / infested
B desired / hired / inspired / transpired
C unimpeded / needed / pleaded / conceded
D delighted / excited / invited / united
E elated / satiated / waited / exaggerated / stated / created /
   hated / evaporated / aggravated
F be-spattered / shattered / tattered / scattered
G smashed / gashed / trashed / slashed
H possessed / confessed / impressed / depressed
I relented / augmented / contented / dissented
J boasted / posted
K wanted / blunted

Task fifty-three

(1) inspired	(11) invited	(21) shattered	(31) aggravated
(2) rested	(12) satiated	(22) slashed	(32) augmented
(3) transpired	(13) rested	(23) depressed	(33) hated
(4) needed	(14) tested	(24) trashed	(34) waited
(5) hired	(15) evaporated	(25) confessed	(35) dissented
(6) pleaded	(16) infested	(26) exaggerated	(36) blunted
(7) excited	(17) scattered	(27) created	(37) posted
(8) conceded	(18) congested	(28) impressed	
(9) united	(19) tattered	(29) stated	
(10) waited	(20) gashed	(30) contented	

Note: (7) could be *united*; (9) could be *excited*; (17) could be *shattered*; (20) could possibly be *slashed*

Task fifty-four

'Noise'

1	whoop	5	roar	9	boom	13	slapping
2	thud	6	throb	10	crash		
3	rattle	7	rush	11	crack		
4	hubbub	8	slam	12	clank		

'Mornings'

1	sheet	5	Bath taps	9	Traffic
2	feet	6	Coffee cups	10	Motor bikes
3	bones	7	Breakfast	11	Power drills
4	Toilets	8	Telephones	12	Jet planes

Task fifty-five

(1) cool	(7) poor	(13) keen	(19) deep
(2) tight	(8) common	(14) strong	(20) steady
(3) sad	(9) happy	(15) rough	(21) strange
(4) blind	(10) proud	(16) fit	
(5) light	(11) bold	(17) thin	
(6) wild	(12) clever	(18) sickly	

Task fifty-six

1 i)	6 r)	11 a)	16 f)
2 l)	7 m)	12 g)	17 n)
3 j)	8 d)	13 k)	18 t)
4 q)	9 p)	14 c)	19 h)
5 b)	10 e)	15 s)	20 o)

Task fifty-seven

1 f)
2 g)
3 a)
4 e)
5 m)
6 d)
7 t)
8 n)
9 r) (in the expression *head over heels in love*)
10 b)
11 c)
12 o)
13 h)
14 j)
15 q)
16 s)
17 l)
18 i)
19 k)
20 p)

Task fifty-eight

1 huffing and puffing
2 higgledy-piggledy
3 high and mighty
4 humdrum
5 by hook or by crook
6 hanky panky
7 hurly burly
8 hunky dory

Completed poems

COMPLETED POEMS

An acrobat is agile

An **ac**robat is agile and can somersault and leap;
An **oc**topus is something you might see beneath the deep.

A **ther**mostat is useful to control the rate of heat;
A **me**tronome is what you need to help you keep the beat.

A **per**iscope is useful if you're in a submarine;
A **chro**mosome is found in living cells, just like a gene.

A **ho**mophone's a word that sounds exactly like another;
A **te**legram is something that you might send to your mother.

A **po**lymorph is something that can take on many shapes;
The **anthropoids** are shaped like us: the monkeys and the apes.

A **te**lephone's for talking to a person far away;
A **mi**crophone can pick up every single word you say.

A **hy**drofoil's a type of boat that skims across the sea;
A **pe**dagogue will teach your little children, for a fee.

A **co**smonaut might visit Venus, Jupiter or Mars;
An **as**tronaut could go much farther, even to the stars.

A **ger**micide is what can help to keep disease at bay;
A **dis**cotheque's for people who like dancing every day.

A **pho**tograph is known to certain people as a 'snap';
A **hyp**notist is someone who could help you take a nap.

A **po**lyglot might understand both Japanese and Czech;
A **ba**thysphere is useful if you want to see a wreck.

The **di**nosaurs all died out 60 million years ago,
while **hy**drogen and **ox**ygen combine as H_2O.

An **aqu**aduct is what will bring you water from afar;
A **via**duct, by contrast, is more useful for your car.

An **au**tograph is written with a pencil or a pen;
A **mo**nocle's occasionally worn by certain men.

A **po**lygraph is something you can use to trap a liar;
and **ae**rosols are things you shouldn't throw into a fire.

A **reg**icide is someone who has killed a queen or king;
(A **mon**archist would never even dream of such a thing).

And if this kind of **lex**icon is hard to comprehend,
then you had better try to get a teacher as a friend.

(See Task seventeen, page 48.)

Down the diner

I was sitting down the diner, toying with my food,
looking at the papers, in a lazy kind of mood

when a little skinny fellow I'd never seen before
came and sat down beside me, and this is what I saw:

my favourite waitress, Sally, came over to the guy
to ask him for his order, and this was his reply:

'I'd like a southern fried chicken, make sure it's really hot,
and a ham and lettuce salad should really hit the spot,

with a thousand island dressing and a touch of blue cheese
then a double western omelette with some sausages and peas,

and a rack or two of ribs with some barbecue sauce
then a king-size burger, with some ketchup, of course.

Can I have the burger in a sesame bun ?
and a good thick rump steak … well-done;

and how about some onions, I like them lightly fried,
with a little piccalilli and some chilli on the side

and I'd like to try a couple of your steak and mushroom pies
with a pile of mashed potato and a plate of french fries

then a salt-beef sandwich − cut it really thick,
with a little French mustard, now that should do the trick.

For dessert I think I'll start with a good old apple pie
with several scoops of ice cream, pile 'em really high;

then a stack of little pancakes with some syrup on top
and an ice cream sundae; perhaps I'd better stop.

No, maybe there's some cheesecake that you can recommend?
OK I'll take the strawberry and that'll be the end.'

So Sally took the order though she thought it was a joke,
then the fellow called her back and said,

'I'd like … a diet coke.'

(See Task thirty, page 79.)

My father's job's more important than yours

My father's job is more **useful** than yours:
He's a doctor who works day and night without **pause**.

My father's job is more **daring** than yours:
He's a stuntman who jumps out of aeroplane **doors**.

My father's job's more **important** than yours:
He's a High Court Judge who helps make the **laws** .

My father's job's more **unusual** than yours:
He's the TV technician who records the **applause**.

My father's job is much **stranger** than yours:
He tames lions and tigers and cuts off their **claws**.

My father's job is more **healthy** than yours:
He's a farmer who spends all his time out of **doors**.

Now, if only your father was as useful as mine:
Then everything here would be perfectly fine!

(See Tasks forty-one and forty-two, page 100.)

Light and shadows by Alan Maley

Inside every saint there's a sinner.
Inside every loser there's a winner.

Inside every **famine** there's a feast.
Inside every lover there's a **beast**.

Inside every **wise** man there's a fool.
Inside every chaos there's a **rule**.

Inside every certainty there's **doubt**.
Inside every **silence** there's a shout.

Inside every death there is **life**.
Inside every **peace** there is strife.

Inside every good man there's a **thief**.
Inside every **worry** there's relief.

Inside every **free** man there's a prisoner.
Inside every chatterbox there's a **listener**.

Inside every general there's a **priest**.
Inside every **most** there's a least.

Inside some **poverty** is wealth.
Inside some sickness there is **health**.

Inside humble acts there is **pride**.
Inside everything we find its other **side**.

(See Task forty-three, page 101.)

Going shopping

Every time she goes out shopping
Mary Williams drives a whopping
great big lorry just to carry all she buys.

For her family's so large
that she really needs a barge
(there are twenty-four of every shape and size).

As she drives her lorry down
to the centre of the town
all the tradesmen start to jump and cheer and shout.

For she spends vast sums of money
just on bread and jam and honey
(not to mention all the wine and beer and stout).

And each day she buys spaghetti
(that's for Margaret, Fred and Betty)
and some mutton chops with very little fat.

And a metre of baloney
with a sack of macaroni
and a tin of something tasty for the cat.

Then there's artichokes and beans
and a case of tinned sardines,
with some anchovies and cabbages and steak.

And especially for Peter
(as he likes things slightly sweeter)
lots of chocolate and a slice or two of cake.

She buys mustard by the pound,
salt and pepper (freshly ground)
and vast quantities of butter, milk and cheese.

And for Cathy, Joe and Reg
(who eat nothing else but veg)
several crates of carrots, radishes and peas.

As for her, what does she eat ?
Is it fish or fruit or meat ?
What's the kind of thing that mothers like the best ?

Well she's got no time for eating
for she's cooking or she's heating
up the food she's bought to serve to all the rest.

(See Task forty-four, page 103.)

Song for London

A The roads are full of potholes
and the streets are full of trash,
the pavements lined with youngsters
asking, 'can you spare some cash ?'

The tubes are packed to bursting
and the buses always late.
If you want to get to town by noon
you'd better leave at eight.

But when the sun is shining
and the river glints like gold,
and the bridges curve like arrows,
then the city takes its hold

and I'm glad to be in London,
though I really can't explain.
And London's where I live
despite the fumes, the dirt and rain.

B The lorries hurtle past me
as I cycle to my work.
If I come home after nightfall
I'm afraid of who might lurk.

You hardly know your neighbours
after 20 years or more,
and use a little spyhole
when someone's at the door

But when I'm sitting waiting
for the concert to begin,
or a play by some young writer
makes me think that we might win,

then I'm glad to be in London,
though it's hard to tell you why.
And London is the city
where I'll live until I die.

C The dogs mess up the pavement,
The kids daren't use the park;
The traffic wrecks the daytime;
alarms disturb the dark.

The rubbish chokes the gutters,
pollution fills the air,
old folks have trouble breathing
and no-one seems to care.

But when I stroll at weekends
through Brick Lane or Camden Town,
I realise that, though
there's plenty here to get me down,

I agree with Doctor Johnson
(though I can't speak for my wife)
that a man who's tired of London
is a man who's tired of life.

(See Tasks forty-six and forty-seven, page 106.)

Failure

He studied so hard but the others all passed.
He tried to be first but he always came last.

He learned Japanese but was transferred to Spain.
He lost his umbrella the day of the rain.

He wore his best suit while the others wore jeans.
He trained as an actor then joined the marines.

He aimed for the yellow but potted the black.
He worked very hard but was given the sack.

He invested in shares then the stock market crashed.
He collected fine china but all of it smashed.

He bought a Picasso which turned out a fake.
He stripped but the weather decided to break.

He held a big party but nobody came.
He hunted a tiger which proved to be tame.

He bought a huge watchdog which just wouldn't bark.
He fished for a salmon but landed a shark.

He played at roulette but he lost every cent.
He opened a cafe but nobody went.

He shot at a pheasant but wounded a wren.
He married a woman who couldn't stand men.

He stuck to the truth while the others all lied.
And so it went on until, sadly, he died.

(See Task forty-eight, page 108.)

Mustn't grumble

'Mustn't grumble', 'Can't complain':
our traditional refrain.
Don't be pushy, best be humble.
Don't complain, and never grumble.

Broken pavings make you stumble?
Cockroach in your apple crumble?
Mustn't grumble, can't complain.

8.05 is late again?
Naughty snowflakes stopped the train?
Don't complain, you shouldn't grumble.

Government begins to fumble?
Housing prices start to tumble?
Mustn't grumble, can't complain.

Trees are killed by acid rain?
BSE attacks the brain?
Don't complain, no need to grumble.

Kiddy's clothes come from the jumble?
Balkan guns begin to rumble?
Do not ask them to explain;
just accept it, don't complain.
Mustn't grumble,
Mustn't grumble,
Mustn't grumble,
Mustn't grumble.

(See Task forty-nine, page 109.)

When the cat's away, the mice will play

A In the Spring my wife suggested
B what she'd secretly desired;
B I agreed it was inspired
A and we'd come back really rested

B So it finally transpired
C that we went off unimpeded,
C kids the last thing that we needed,
B in the caravan we'd hired.

C So they cried and wept and pleaded?
D Course they didn't; all delighted
D they accepted, quite excited.
C 'Good for you', the lads conceded.

D 'Off you go!' they said, united;
E so we drove off, quite elated,
E while they phoned (they might have waited!)
D to the various friends invited.

E Three weeks later, satiated,
A we returned, completely rested,
A but our patience soon was tested
E and our joy evaporated.

A For the house was mouse-infested,
F rooms uncleaned, the walls be-spattered,
F sinks unwashed and dishes scattered,
A everywhere with kids congested.

F Curtains all completely tattered;
G telly, CD, video smashed;
G all my records warped and gashed;
F glasses, windows, all were shattered

G Sunday clothes were ripped and slashed
H by some fool no doubt possessed
H (or else clinically depressed);
G all the house completely trashed!

H Deeply shamed the boys confessed
E they'd indeed exaggerated,
E loathed the chaos they'd created.
H We, however, quite impressed

E by their demeanour simply stated
I that we had indeed relented.
I Fact is, secretly contented,
E we were far from aggravated

I and were pleased, our joy augmented
E by the thought that we both hated
E all our things, indeed had waited
I to replace them. None dissented,

J all agreed, in fact we boasted
K of the marvellous things we wanted;
K but our happiness was blunted:
J uninsured – the cheque not posted!

(See Task fifty-two, page 111.)

Noise by Jessie Pope

I like noise.
The whoop of the boy, the thud of a hoof,
the rattle of rain on a galvanised roof.
the hubbub of traffic, the roar of a train,
the throb of machinery numbing the brain,
the switching of wires in an overhead tram,
the rush of the wind, a door on the slam,
the boom of the thunder, the crash of the waves,
the din of a river that races and raves,
the crack of a rifle, the clank of a pail,
the strident tattoo of a swift–slapping sail.
From any old sound that the silence destroys
arises a gamut of soul–stirring joys.
I like noise.

Mornings by Alan Maley

Rustling **sheet**,
Shuffling **feet**,
Creaking **bones**,
Stifled groans,
Chirping, crowing,
Noses blowing,
Toilets flushing,
Bath taps gushing,
Coffee cups clatter,
Breakfast chatter,
Neighbours singing,
Telephones ringing,
Radios tuning,
Traffic booming,
Motor bikes thrumming,
Power drills drumming,
Jet planes thunder –
I just wonder
at the NOISE!

(See Task fifty-four, page 116.)

Sensible similes

As white as a lily, as blue as the sky,
as bright as the flags on the Fourth of July.

As cool as a cucumber, tight as a drum,
as sad as a child falling flat on its bum.

As blind as a bat, as light as a feather,
as wild as a horse at the end of its tether.

As poor as a church mouse, as common as muck,
as happy as Chinamen dining on duck.

As proud as a peacock, as bold as brass,
as clever as kids who are top of the class.

As keen as mustard, as strong as an ox,
as rough as a rocker with long, filthy locks.

As fit as a fiddle, as thin as a rake,
as sickly as icing on top of a cake.

As deep as the ocean, as steady as time,
as strange as a simile used in a rhyme.

(See Task fifty-five, page 133.)